1

Campaigns
Of
38th Regiment
Illinois Volunteer Infantry
Company — K—
Enlisted at Newton
Jasper County Illinois
July 27th A.D. 1861
Organized Monday July 28th
by electing William C. Harris
Captain, G. W. Johnson
First Lieutenant,
Isaiah Foster Second Lieutenant
The Company left Newton
Monday August 12th about
11 O'clock A. M. the day was
Cloudy, and drizzling rain till
about 10. P. M.

...arrived at Olney about 6 P.M.
Staid at the "Brillhart" House.
August 13th We left Olney at
2 O'clock A.M. on the train
for Camp Butler and stopped
at Sandoval at 7 A.M.
where we remained till 1 A.M.
of the 14th waiting for a train
we stopped again at Decatur
at 10 A.M. took breakfast
at the Revere House and left
at 3 P.M. in Company with
Captain Carmichael's Company
from Mason County.
We arrived at Camp Butler
at 5 P.M. and went into Camp
Camp Butler is located on the
east bank of Clear Lake, 6 miles
east of Springfield and 2 miles
south of Jamestown

JASPER COUNTY YANKEE

CAMPAIGNS *of the* 38TH REGIMENT,
ILLINOIS VOLUNTEER INFANTRY,
COMPANY K

WRITTEN BY
William Elwood Patterson
1861–1863

EDITED BY
Lowell Wayne Patterson, Ed.D.

HERITAGE BOOKS
2011

HERITAGE BOOKS
AN IMPRINT OF HERITAGE BOOKS, INC.

Books, CDs, and more—Worldwide

For our listing of thousands of titles see our website
at
www.HeritageBooks.com

Published 2011 by
HERITAGE BOOKS, INC.
Publishing Division
100 Railroad Ave. #104
Westminster, Maryland 21157

This book was previously published as:

*Campaigns of the 38th Regiment of the Illinois Volunteer Infantry
Company K, 1861–1863: The Diary of Elwood Patterson*

1981

International Standard Book Numbers
Paperbound: 978-0-7884-5306-9
Clothbound: 978-0-7884-8731-6

JASPER COUNTY YANKEE

THE DIARY

W. E. Patterson's Diary was originally written in a small booklet of approximately 94 pages covered with cardboard and marbleized paper. In 1981, one hundred years later, its pages were dismantled, deacidified and encapsulated. The whole was then rebound in leather and given a leather slipcase in order to preserve the contents for future generations.

Apparently, some of the entries found in this diary were made on the battlefield soon after the battle, while others may have been added later when he returned home from the war and read his own letters that he had sent to his father and mother.

Contents

Contents

JASPER COUNTY YANKEE

INTRODUCTION

William Elwood Patterson was born April 4, 1841 on the Patterson Plantation at Sandy Creek, Randolph County, North Carolina. When he was a boy of nine or ten years of age, his parents decided to move to Jasper County, Illinois.

Before the Civil War changed his life, William's principal occupation was teacher; but, after he returned from the war, he was a farmer, and served the citizens of Jasper County, Illinois as Justice of the Peace, and Notary Public. During his teaching career, before the war, he was privileged to teach Lawrence Y. Sherman (senator from Illinois). All four of William's children were teachers. He purchased the first school bell in Jasper County, Illinois in 1858. This hand bell was used by his four children and later passed down to succeeding generations. The school bell was last rung by Dr. Lowell W. Patterson, in the schools of Hawkins County, Tennessee in 1988. It has since been restored and now rests in the Elmer Julian Patterson Archives in Rogersville, Tennessee.

This diary will note that while in the Union Army, William's travels took him through Illinois, Missouri, Arkansas, Mississippi, Tennessee, and Kentucky. He fought in many battles and was wounded at Chickamauga on September 19, 1863. The original diary is kept in the Elmer Julian Archives.

An old note from the archives gives this statement: W.E. Patterson was born near Julian, Randolph County, North Carolina on April 4th, 1841. Passed from this life at 1:54 P.M. on February 17, 1916. He came to Illinois with his parents when about nine or ten years of age. On the twelfth day of August, 1861 he enlisted in Company K, 38th Illinois Volunteers and served till close of war when he was honorably discharged (was wounded four times at Chickamauga). He was converted and joined the Methodist Church when a young man and...(lost part of document).

PREFACE & ACKNOWLEDGMENTS

The first person to be acknowledged here should, of course, be the original author, William Elwood Patterson. Aside from his accomplishments that are listed in the introduction to this narrative, he must have been a caring man, a man of far-reaching sensibilities, a man who sensed the importance of his existence in the scheme of things. Subsequent generations have been honored because he took the time to write down, in careful detail, his impressions of exactly what transpired during *his* Civil War.

Then, I would like to acknowledge my wife Barbara for her patience, advice, and encouragement during the course of this project. Also her brother, Dr. Raymond Corice, Jr. who is a professor at Hinds Community College in Mississippi, who has helped edit and proofread the accompanying document. He has also provided very timely and important "computer-wise" suggestions that have saved time and errors in the final production phase of this project.

And lastly, I would like to acknowledge Ellen Addison, editor of the Rogersville Review, and her husband Ben, for help in setting up copy and photographs for this book version of the diary.

Lowell W. Patterson, BS, MA, EdD

Rogersville, Tennessee

CHAPTER I

Jasper County, Illinois

JULY, 1861

These are the Campaigns of the 38th Regiment, Illinois Volunteer Infantry, Company K. Enlisted at Newton, Jasper County Illinois, July 27th, A.D. 1861. Organized Monday, July 29th by electing William C. Harris Captain, G. W. Johnson 1st Lieutenant, Isaiah Foster 2nd Lieutenant. The company left Newton Monday, August 12th about 11 o'clock A.M. The day was cloudy and drizzling rain till about 10 A.M.

Arrived at Olney about 6 P.M. Stayed at the Brillhart House. August 13th we left Olney at 2 o'clock A.M. on the train for Camp Butler and stopped at Sandoval at 7 A.M. where we remained till 1 A.M. of the 14th, waiting for another train. We stopped again at Decatur at 10 A.M., took breakfast at the Revere House and left at 3 P.M. in company with Captain Carmichael's Company from Massac County. We arrived at Camp Butler at 5 P.M. and went into camp. Camp Butler is located on the east bank of Clear Lake, 6 miles east of Springfield and 2 miles south of Pinetown.

The members of this company (including both

original volunteers and recruits) were as follows: Captain W. C. Harris 1st Lieutenant, G. W. Johnson 2nd Lieutenant, Zed Foster, John and Joe Allison, Nicholas Andom, Jno and Lewis Brooks, Michael and David Bowers, Tower and Lindsay Bostick, William and Oliver Babbs, Allison Black, Alex B. Batman, Raleigh M. Brackett, Boss M. Bridges, Roberts Benefield, Benjamin Bogard, Jno Chestnut, Frank Carter, William Colvin, Martin Christian, James D. Devine, Jonah F. Debolt, Jno Francis, Jonathon Foster, James E. Freeman, Job Fithian, Elzy Dobbins, Richard Elder, A. P. Berlin, Henry L. and Jno G. Bliss, Jno Bixler, Jonas Fiesey, Matthew H. Bridges, Jerry Holm, Joe W. Harris, A. I. Irving, Ithamas Clark, Jno L. Jones, William Jordan, Joe Kinney, G. W. Hibler, Jno W. Lee, William Lord, Decatur Mondon, Jno McDowell, William Martin, H. P. and Joe P. Moulden, Henry C. Moore, Minor Mitchell, Kenneth Newton, W. E. Patterson, Joseph Powell, Robert Ping, N. B. Parker, J. A. Reed, D. W. Richards, Frederic Rotzler, Frederic Rosebalt, Wickham Ryan, Lewis G. Riggin, Joe Shedelbauer, G. W. Sutton, William Sutton, P. N. and Sam Scott, Jonathon and Jno Trexler, George V. Vanderhogg, John Mulvany, William and Elijah Worthy, Anderson Burnside, Ross Welch and William Welch, Zebulon P. Wheeler and A. Wheeler, Bushrod W. Harris, John (Zug) Hagerman, Nathan Cathers, Jackson Selby, Martin B. Hawkins, George Hensly, Benjamin Stallings, David B. Hankins [Hawkins} and Avery Hankins, Powell Walters, Elias (Pony) Walters, John R. Malcolm, Joe McNair, Lew Four, Martin B. Wilson, George Stockwell, Michael Stockwell, Isaac Smith, Cyrus J. Brewer, Eliphaz Reisner, Stephen Richards, Jacob E.

Reed, and Sydney Kibler.

We were mustered into the United States service Saturday morning, August 17th, by Colonel Pitcher, Commander of the Camp, and sworn to obey the Constitution of the United States, the President and our superior officers for the term of three years unless sooner discharged. The company was first organized in the 26th Illinois Regiment commanded by Colonel Loomis as Company H. It was subsequently transferred to the 38th Regiment Illinois Volunteer Infantry as Company K. The regimental officers of this regiment were Colonel William P. Carlin, Lieutenant-Colonel Mortimer O'Kean, Major Daniel Gilmer, Adjutant W. Willet, Quartermaster F. Fuller, Surgeon Teed, Assistant Surgeon Stewart, Sergeant Major Sturgis.

On September 18th, the 38th Regiment Illinois Volunteers received orders to prepare to leave Camp Butler for parts unknown. On the 19th we struck tents and packed up, and on the morning of the 20th formed in line of battle on the drill-ground and marched out of Camp Butler at sunrise, took passage on a train of flat cars at Pinctown and went to Alton. There we were transferred to the deck of the David Tatum and went to St. Louis. We passed the night in the cabin of the L. M. Hennett and, on the morning of the 21st, started on the Iron Mountain Railroad to Pilot Knob, Iron County, Missouri. We arrived at Pilot Knob at dark of that day and passed the night on the ground where we got off the train. Here, for the first time, the rocks were our bed and our covering the sky, and said rocks were sufficiently hard to cause us to realize for the first time that we were soldiers.

On Sunday morning, September 22nd, we pitched our camp in a field between Shepherd's Mountain and the town of Pilot Knob, Missouri. The force at this place consisted of the 21st Illinois at Ironton, 33rd Illinois at Arcadia, 38th Illinois and 1st Indiana Cavalry at Pilot Knob, all under the command of Colonel W. P. Carlin of the 38th.

On October 14th, a rebel force made their appearance in the neighborhood of Potosi and, on the morning of the 15th, burnt Big River Bridge and skedaddled. About dark on the evening of the 14th, a detachment of the 38th, consisting of companies A, I, and K (commanded by Major Gilmer), started to Potosi and, on the 15th, went to the bridge, found it burnt and returned to camp. Company F was then sent to the bridge to remain as guards.

On the 17th, the 1st Indiana Cavalry was engaged in a skirmish with Jeff Thompson's command at Fredericktown and retreated with the loss of 3 men wounded. At 3 o'clock P.M. the 38th, 33rd and 21st marched out towards Fredericktown and met the cavalry returning 10 miles from Ironton. We then returned to camp, arriving at the Knob at midnight. The 8th Wisconsin Infantry and 1st Missouri Battery had arrived in our absence.

On October 20th, at 2 P.M., Carlins' command again started to Fredericktown, leaving the post in charge of the sick and convalescents. We marched nearly all night and arrived at Fredericktown on the 21st where **they** were joined by Colonel Plummer's command from Cape Girardeau. The rebels, under Jeff Thompson and Colonel Lowe, had left the town before our men arrived. The Union forces marched through the town and found the rebels in position about 2 miles from Fredericktown. An immediate attack was made and carried on for some time by the artillery and a part of the infantry. The battle was ended by the 1st Indiana Calvary charging upon the rebel line. Major Gavit of that regiment was killed while leading the charge in advance of his regiment. The rebels retreated, leaving 400 men on the field amongst whom was Colonel Lowe, one of their commanders. The command returned to Pilot Knob on the 25th.

Early in November, the 21st Illinois, 8th Wisconsin, 1st Indiana Cavalry, and 1st Missouri Battery started on an expedition to the St. Francois River in command of Colonel Carlin. On the 7th the 38th received marching orders and, on the 9th marched at 6 A.M., commanded by Lieutenant Colonel O'Kean. That evening we camped at Marble Springs, which is 12 miles from the Knob. On the 10th we marched 13 miles and camped at Bailey's Tavern. On the 11th we marched 18 miles and camped on Hardee's Camping Ground that is near Greenville on the St. Francois River. On the morning of the 12th, Colonel Carlin, with the balance of the command (excepting the 33rd which remained at Arcadia), arrived at Greenville. On their return from Poplar Bluffs and Indian Ford they had captured 15 prisoners as a result of the expedition.

The whole command started to the Knob on the morning of the 13th. That night we camped near Patterson. On the 14th we marched 13 miles and camped in a creek bottom between Bailey's Tavern and Marble Creek. On the 15th we arrived at the Knob at 2 o'clock P.M. On the 25th the 8th

Wisconsin (or Live Eagle regiment) left Pilot Knob for Sulphur Springs, near St. Louis. The other regiments went into winter quarters. The 21st erected winter quarters at Fort Alexander near Ironton, the 33rd at Fort Hovey near Arcadia, and the 38th moved further up the valley to the north of the town and drew Sybley tents. Company F was at Big River Bridge. Company K erected log-cabins west of the main camp. The cavalry and battery drew tents and remained in the valley.

Besides the battery, there were 3 pieces of heavy artillery stationed at the Knob; one on the Ironton Road, one on the Caledonia Road, and one on the top of Pilot Knob Mountain. On the 27th of December there was a review of troops at this post at Arcadia by the Inspector General Van Rensaler. From this time till March nothing of importance transpired at this place. Christmas was duly honored by the 38th Illinois Volunteers, undersigned was unfortunately on picket.

CHAPTER II

Missouri to Alabama

NEW YEAR'S DAY, 1862

New Year's Day, 1862 was ushered in by a salute from the battery. Sometime in the month of January the regiments at this post received orders to return all extra baggage and prepare for a campaign and about the last of January the 21st Illinois went to Greenville. On the third of March the 38th left Pilot Knob.

At this time our once very full company had been very much reduced by disease and death. Dyson Dyer died at Camp Butler. Z.P. Wheeler, A.P. Selby, Martin B. Hawkins, George Hensley and Powell Walters died at Pilot Knob. The bodies of Wheeler and Walters were sent home. The others were buried in the graveyard on the Farmington Road. Lieutenant Foster resigned his commission about the last of January, or early in February, and Peter Neal Scott was unanimously elected 2nd Lieutenant of Company K. On January 22nd, Washington Johnson had relinquished his position at Camp Butler and Bush W. Harris had received the commission of 1st Lieutenant.

On the 6th of March, the 38th arrived at Patterson, undersigned being left in the hospital at Ironton. On the 9th they marched to Reves' Station on Black River which is ned by Captain Mitchell (who was afterwards killed at Vicksburg). The 2nd Brigade was commanded by Colonel Hovey of the 33rd Illinois (or Normal Regiment), the 3rd Brigade by Colonel Brown of the 1st Indiana Cavalry.

On Monday, March 31st, a number of us who had been left at the Knob sick, started with a provision train towards our regiment. William Colvin, A.J. Irving, Stephen Richards and Isaac Smith and Martin B. Wilson had been discharged from the service. We arrived at Black River on Wednesday, April 2nd. Having had the pleasure of being run over by an army wagon on April 1st, I felt slightly fatigued in consequence.

We remained at Reves' Station on the 3rd and, on Friday April 4th, we started to Doniphan. Had a very rough road over hills and swamps. Went 18 miles and camped on the edge of a swamp near an old mill (Pondy's). It rained very hard that night. I slept under a wagon, had a good time. On April 5th we arrived at Doniphan and rejoined our companies.

On April 6th our ed by Captain Mitchell (who was afterwards killed at Vicksburg). The 2nd Brigade was commanded by Colonel Hovey of the 33rd Illinois (or Normal Regiment), the 3rd Brigade by Colonel Brown of the 1st Indiana Cavalry.

On Monday, March 31st, a number of us who had been left at the Knob sick, started with a provision train towards our regiment. William Colvin, A.J. Irving, Stephen Richards and Isaac Smith and Martin

B. Wilson had been discharged from the service. We arrived at Black River on Wednesday, April 2nd. Having had the pleasure of being run over by an army wagon on April 1st, I felt slightly fatigued in consequence.

We remained at Reves' Station on the 3rd and, on Friday April 4th, we started to Doniphan. Had a very rough road over hills and swamps. Went 18 miles and camped on the edge of a swamp near an old mill (Pondy's). It rained very hard that night. I slept under a wagon, had a good time. On April 5th we arrived at Doniphan and rejoined our companies.

On April 6th our pickets at the ferry were fired upon from the opposite side of the river at about 9 or 10 o'clock at night, by some of Tim Reves' men (it was supposed). Six shots were fired. Mitchell's Battery then shelled the woods. The infantry were formed in line and the cavalry crossed the river, but without result. On April 8th, the ferry boat being built here was finished, and Companies K (of the 38th) and the 21st crossed the river at dark and explored the neighborhood. We returned to camp about midnight. A great many citizens came in while we remained here to take the oath of allegiance. Tim Reves, meanwhile, was keeping our pickets stirred up.

On the 16th, Carlin's Brigade left Doniphan, crossed Current River, and marched towards Pocahontas. On the 18th we camped at a mill on Fauchet Duman (Fosha Duman) Creek. We remained at Fauchet Duman 2 days. The weather was rainy, road muddy, muchly so.

On the 21st we marched to Pocahontas, Randolph County, Arkansas. One man, belonging to the 5th

Illinois Cavalry, was killed by guerrillas three miles from the town, his regiment being in the advance. Van Dorn, who commanded here, had evacuated before our arrival and gone to Jacksonport. On the 23rd we moved camp 1 mile west of Pocahontas. On the 30th we left Pocahontas, marched 10 miles and camped on Black River.

On May 1st we crossed Black River on a flat boat which was pressed into the service at Pocahontas and brought down the river to this place by Company I. We marched 4 miles further and camped. On May 2nd our march took us through several cypress swamps. We camped on the premises of one of the natives near a swamp pond. On the 3rd we encountered more cypress swamps. We crossed a bilious-looking creek in the heart of a cypress swamp called Running Water. Then we camped at a log-cabin church 8 miles from Jacksonport, where an Arkansas preacher was holding forth to some of the natives. The congregation, especially the ladies, manifested some surprise at our sudden appearance by screaming at the top of their voices. They evidently thought that the Day of Kingdom Come was at hand. On May 4th we arrived at Jacksonport and camped on the banks of White River.

On May 10th, the 21st and 38th Illinois started to Gape Girardeau, Missouri, leaving the 2nd Brigade and General Curtis' command at Jacksonport. We marched 27 miles on the 10th and marched and camped on the bank of a lake in a cypress swamp near the residence of the same individual on whose premises we had camped as we went down. On the 11th we marched 25 miles and camped near a creek close to another swamp. May 12th we arrived at Pocahontas. On the 13th we camped at Pitman's Ferry on Current River. On May 14th we crossed the river, the men by swimming, the baggage train on a boat, and camped on the bank of the river. Two men were drowned in crossing the river. On the 15th we marched to Pondy's Mill. On the 16th we were at Reves' Station again, camped about a mile north of the station. May 17th we marched to Greenville on the St. Francois and camped on the bank of the river. On the 18th we marched to Fox Creek, and on the 19th camped 27 miles from Cape Girardeau. On the May 20th we marched at 4 A.M. It rained all the time till about noon. We waded White Water and arrived at Cape Girardeau at 1 o'clock P.M.

On May 21st, Jeff C. Davis' Brigade arrived at Cape Girardeau. We were paid off by the Paymaster here and, in the evening, went on board the Steamer Empress. On May 22nd we were on our way to Corinth, Mississippi. We laid over that night at Fort Henry on the Tennessee River. On the night of the 23rd we were at Pittsburg Landing. On the 24th we landed at Hamburg Landing, Tennessee. On the 26th we marched from Hamburg and camped near Farmington, Mississippi, about 3 miles from the Union lines in front of Corinth.[1]

On the morning of the 28th the artillery opened heavily along the lines with sharp musketry firing along the center and left. At 9 A.M. the long roll was beat and we started for the lines and took our positions in rifle pits on the extreme left in Pope's Division with the 21st Illinois and 1st Missouri Battery. Cannonading was heard at intervals with heavy infantry skirmishing. This kept up till the 30th. On the 30th the rebels evacuated Corinth. On the 31st we marched through the rebel works and camped near Price's Camp which lies 3 miles from Corinth. A heavy skirmish took place at Tuscumbia River on the 31st, about 3 miles south of our camp.

On June 3rd we marched to Danville and, on the 4th marched back and camped near the Tuscumbia River. The next 2 days we spent rebuilding the Tuscumbia River Bridge, which the rebs had torn down. On the 7th, we marched to Pope's division camp near Booneville, and, on the 12th marched back to Tuscumbia River. On the 13th we marched to Clear Creek, which is 4 or 5 miles from Corinth, and went into camp. We remained here till June 23rd. William Martin died here and was buried in the pine woods close to camp on the Jacinto Road. We left Clear Creek on the 23rd and arrived at Jacinto, the county seat of Tishomingo County, on the 24th. We marched towards Holly Springs. The expedition consisted of Brigadier Generals Jeff C. Davis and Hamilton Beaufort, and Sullivan's Division under the command of General Asboth. On the 29th we arrived at Ripley and, on the 30th (at 4 P.M.), Davis' Division marched towards Holly Springs and camped 10 miles from Ripley.

On July 1st we marched back to Ripley where, on that morning (from some cause known only in official circles), the expedition commenced a precipitate retreat towards Corinth. Davis' Division returned to Ripley and there burned the greater portion of our tents and extra baggage. Then we marched on for 7 miles further and camped. On the

2nd we continued our march to Rienzi, arriving at the place late at night, very much fatigued. We remained at Rienzi on the 3rd and on the Fourth of July, 1862 marched to Jacinto and went into camp about 2 miles east of the town, where we remained till August 14th. Upon our arrival here, our brigade was augmented by the addition of the 15th Wisconsin Infantry, a regiment of Norwegians commanded by Colonel Heg, and the 2nd Minnesota Battery commanded by Captain Hotchkiss. Carlins' was at this time the 2nd Brigade, 4th Division, Army of the Mississippi. Brigadier General Jeff C. Davis was division commander.

Nothing of interest transpired while we remained here. We occasionally heard from General Sterling Price, but he did not cultivate a close acquaintance. Our near neighbor and friend at this place was Colonel Davenport, a secesh gentleman with two sons in the rebel army. We guarded his property, devoured his fruit and confiscated 2 or 3 of his juvenile Negroes.

On August 14th we left Jacinto and marched 9 miles and camped. We left camp at Jacinto at 4 P.M. On the 15th we arrived at Iuka and camped about 1 mile from Iuka Springs. We remained here till the 21st, then marched to Eastport on the Tennessee River. We camped on the bank of the river, and, on the 22nd, crossed the river and camped on the opposite bank. General Robert Mitchell took command of the division at Eastport, General Davis being absent. We were joined also by the 8th Kansas Infantry; Lieutenant Colonel O'Kean commanding the 38th, Colonel Carlin commanding the 2nd Brigade.

On August 23rd we started for Florence, Alabama. We camped late in the night in a field of young cotton. On the 24th we camped at Martins Factory, a most attractive place in many respects, situated on a beautiful stream and in a rough and hilly locality. On the 25th we arrived at Florence at about 8 or 10 o'clock A.M. Florence is the most beautiful town in this part of the Southern Confederacy. It is on the Tennessee River, opposite Tuscumbia. Here is where Douglass was egged in 1860. August 26th we commenced the hardest march we ever undertook in all our campaigns during three years service. We left everything we could dispense with and, with 20 days rations in the train, started towards Nashville Tennessee. That night we camped near a small creek. Charley Martin of Company I was shot here through the leg by the accidental discharge of a gun in camp. He died later from the effects of the wound.

CHAPTER III

Alabama to Kentucky by way of Tennessee

AUGUST, 1862

On August 27th we camped near Lawrenceburg in an old field the opposite side of the creek from the town. On that same day some heavy-complected individuals who joined us in Alabama became disgusted with their new-found freedom and returned to the "flesh pots of Egypt."

On the 28th we camped near Mt. Pleasant in a beautiful grove in a country abounding in melons and other forage. On the following day we camped opposite Columbia on Duck River. The next evening we camped near Triune, having left the Nashville Road that day at Franklin. About 1 o'clock the camp was aroused by a report that a rebel force with artillery were about to attack us. We formed in line and silently marched out to await the attack. We remained under arms till morning, when it was ascertained that the cause of the alarm was a wagon loaded with cotton which had broken down near our camp and which the fertile imaginations of our pickets had transformed into a rebel battery. The profane remarks of the contraband driver sounded to their lively apprehensions like the commands of an artillery officer.

The next day we arrived at Murfreesboro and camped on the banks of Stones River. On September 3rd we started to Nashville at 5 P.M., did not go into camp that night at all, and the next day camped about 3 miles from Nashville, east of the road. We remained here till the 7th. In the meantime General Alexander McCook's division passed us and went on to Nashville, followed by a host of contrabands of all ages and sexes, but all in a destitute condition. That celebrated individual, "Intelligent Contraband," was not of their number.

On the 7th we marched through Nashville, crossed the Cumberland River, and camped at Edgfield, opposite Nashville. On September 9th the 38th was ordered out on a scout, a squad of rebels having made their appearance in the neighborhood. We marched out on the pike leading to Bowling Green and halted for an hour or two. While we remained here, Andrew Johnson, military governor of Tennessee, passed us, riding along in his buggy. We then turned to the right and marched north, then east, then north and passed through a large plantation directly, past the house and then in the river bottom where an American Citizen of African descent informed us the rebels were gone. We explored the neighborhood, found nary enemy, and returned to camp.

On September 11th at 3 P.M., we started on the march to Louisville, Kentucky; McCooks' division and other forces having passed us at Edgfield. About dark a violent rain storm came up. It rained very hard with thunder and lightning, and was very dark. We arrived at Edgefield Junction about 12 o'clock noon and went into camp. This place is the junction of the Louisville and Nashville and the Clarksville Railroads, and is 10 miles from Nashville. On the 12th, Company K was on picket on the turnpike leading towards Galatine. We marched about 1 or 2 P.M. and camped near Tybee Springs, having marched till late, and crossed the White Hills. In crossing these hills a caisson belonging to the 2nd Minnesota Battery was upset down the side of the mountain, but without serious injury to anyone.

Company K was on rear guard when that amiable and beloved officer, Colonel Pease (provost marshal of the division), made his appearance in our midst as we arrived in the neighborhood of camp and put us on picket again. It seems that a member of Company K, neglecting to show a proper amount of devotion at his august appearance, was placed under arrest by that military genius.

On the 13th we marched about 3 o'clock in the morning. We halted about 4 o'clock P.M., marched back 1 mile and camped in an orchard. On the morning of the 14th reveille was at half past one, and we marched at 2 A.M. We camped in a grove in which were a number of sink holes. One of these sink holes was filled nearly to the top with water and presented the appearance of a mere fissure in a bed of rock. From this we obtained water while we remained here. A contraband, in descending upon these rocks to get to the water, lost his footing and disappeared from view and was probably drowned as he never reappeared to tell the tale. Upon retiring to our humble couches we were officially notified that reveille would be beat at 2 o'clock which was carried out to the very letter.

On September 15th we marched at 2? A.M., and overtook McCook's division 4 miles from Bowling Green. We arrived at Bowling Green about noon. We went into camp about a mile northwest of Bowling Green near Barren River. Davis' division was now attached to the division of General Alexander McDowell McCook. On the 17th, the National forces under the command of Major General Don Carlos Buell left Bowling Green in pursuit of the rebel army commanded by General Braxton Bragg, which was marching towards Louisville.

Mitchell's division, as we were then called, left Bowling Green on the 17th, waded Barren River and marched towards Glasgow. The main army marched directly towards Louisville, leaving the supply train at Bowling Green to follow at its leisure. We captured a rebel picket post near Glasgow and camped 8 miles from the town.

The next day, September 18th, we marched towards Mumfordsville to rejoin the main army which had overtaken Bragg near Green River and were in line of battle expecting an engagement. We camped that night on the Bowling Green Pike near Bell's Tavern. About this time our rations began to diminish and continued to grow beautifully less, until in a few days our supply played out entirely.

On the 19th we advanced about a mile and a half and took our position on the railroad about 3 miles from the scene of action. Buell's army remained in line of battle near Cafe City till the 21st; the generals harassing the enemy in the meantime by a vast amount of flagging through the signal corps. In this way he "rendered signal service to the country."

On the 20th, 3 days rations of hard tack and pickled pork were issued to us, the last we got till we got to Louisville. On the 21st Bragg moved on towards Louisville, and after giving him a few hours the advance, Buell started in pursuit. We marched on the morning of the 21st for 3 miles and halted on the late disputed territory at a large and deep cave a mile or two east of Cave City. We remained here till near night, then marched again. We marched very hard till late at night. The campfires greeted our weary visions about 10 or 11 o'clock that night. We went into camp 7 miles from Mumfordsville in a field of corn that was just beginning to ripen. Our rations being short, we made gritters of our tin plates and reduced said corn to meal, which we baked before the fires on boards.

On September 22nd, we marched at 3 P.M. and crossed Green River that night, passing deserted camp fires for several miles after crossing the river. We marched all night, not halting till next morning at 6 o'clock when we obtained a barrel of flour and worms in pretty equal proportions. Having no means of separating the flour from the worms, we made them up into flap-jacks and devoured them with much relish. After devoting about an hour to the flap-jacks, we marched with renewed vigor. We marched rapidly all day, and about 10 o'clock arrived at Elizabethtown, where our division went into camp. We then marched around in all possible directions for an hour, hunting our proper position in the brigade. We found it by about 11 o'clock P.M. in an extremely weedy field; stacked our arms and sank down in our places into the arms of "kind nature's sweet restorer, balmy sleep," the first we had since the night of the 21st, having marched hard for 32 hours with only one meal in the time. At this camp two Irishmen of Company C (of the 38th) got into a difficulty and one of them deliberately shot the other dead upon the spot. The murdered man was buried here, but his murderer got off with but very light punishment, if any, and afterwards returned to duty in his company.

On September 24th we marched at about 6 o'clock. We camped about 9 o'clock that night at West Point on the Ohio River. Received some more flour sufficient for our suppers. On the 25th, reveille came at an early hour. The rebel army had turned to the right, directly on to Louisville. We camped on the night of the 25th on the Ohio River, 11 miles below Louisville at about sunset. Some fresh beef was issued to us here for our suppers, which we roasted by the campfires, and devoured with salt. Had Patrick Henry appeared in our camp at that time he might, with propriety, have exclaimed, "Beef! Beef! Beef!

At about 1 o'clock at night our slumbers were disturbed by the beating of the drums, and we received orders to prepare to march. We hastily took our arms, and prepared to "take up our beds and walk." We stood in line 15 or 20 minutes when, to our inexpressible relief, the order was countermanded, and we again sought repose within the comfortable folds of our blankets to dream of home and the balmy days of peace when the sound of the long roll was "not heard in the land."

On September 26th, we marched at about 6 or 7 o'clock A.M. We arrived at Louisville, Kentucky about 2 P.M., marched through the city, and camped on the "Point;" and here ended the hardest march we ever endured. With only a few days intermission at Murfreesboro, Nashville, and Bowling Green; our march extended from Florence, Alabama to Louisville, Kentucky; a forced march of about 306 miles direct. But, as we came, via Murfreesboro and Glasgow, about 350 miles, with water very scarce, roads extremely dusty, weather hot and rations short. From the 19th to the evening of the 26th we received but 3 days rations, exclusive of the beforementioned flour and beef. We were traveling night and day in close proximity to our hostile fellow citizens of Bragg's command. While we were marching, almost naked and barefoot, often at dead of night; the solitudes of the forest would ring with sonorous imprecations on "Old Buell" by the exhausted soldiers whose resentment found vent in curses upon a leader in whom they had no confidence and to whose neglect of duty they ascribed the sufferings of this march.

We were met with a cordial welcome at Louisville by the citizens who, but the day before, were trembling with apprehension at the near approach of the rebel army. We remained at Louisville 4 days. The army was largely reinforced at Louisville and reorganized. Carlin's Brigade was increased by the addition of the 101st Ohio Infantry. It now consisted of the 21st Illinois on the right of the brigade, 15th Wisconsin next, 101st Ohio next (commanded by Colonel Stern), and the 38th Illinois on the left. It was known as the 32nd Brigade, 9th Division, 3rd Army Corps, General Gilbert Corps Commander.

While we were at Louisville, General Davis (who had returned to take command of our division) killed General Nelson and, in consequence of this event, General Robert B. Mitchell retained command of Davis' Division. And well would it have been for said division if the same weapon that killed Nelson had wound the wild career of Davis to a close at the same time.

On October 1st we left Louisville in search of General Bragg. We marched but a short distance; it was very hot. The 101sters were about played out. We camped to the right of the road. We were ordered to burn no rails, and told that we might burn pieces. Consequently, we found plenty of pieces. On the 2nd we marched very deliberately. The 101sters were very tired, and began throwing away blankets and clothes. The 38th picked them up. We camped in the woods. A gang of sheep roamed into our camp. The 101sters went for them. 101sters learnt a lesson in regard to foraging, old soldiers amused.

On the 3rd we were called up at 3 o'clock. We stood in line till daylight, stacked arms and got our breakfasts. We camped early that evening on the bank of Salt River near one of Buell's signal stations. Other camps were in place further up the valley. On the 4th we drew rations, marched at 7 or 8 o'clock in the rain. We camped at the foot of a hill near a creek. Hotchkiss' Battery, belonging to Carlin's Brigade, took position on the hill, ready for action.

On October 5th we arrived at Bardstown at 7 or 8 o'clock P.M. We camped a mile from the town in a field. We demolished the plank fence nearby, as the night was cool. On the 6th we marched tolerably early, soon after daylight. We camped near Springfield in a field about a half mile to the left of the road. On the 7th we marched till about 7 or 8 o'clock and placed our knapsacks, blankets, etc. in the train which was not to come up again till about the 18th.

CHAPTER IV

The Battle of Chaplin Hills Perryville, Kentucky

OCTOBER, 1862

The Battle of Chaplin Hills commenced about 2 o'clock P.M. Our advance came up with the enemy on the hills of Chaplin Creek near Perryville.[2] Bragg had taken his position on the hills to the left of Perryville, having Chaplin Creek in his rear, his left wing extending to the town. Davis' (or Mitchell's) division had arrived within 37 miles of Perryville on the Perryville Road, when the boom of a cannon (the first gun fired in the Battle of Chaplin Hills) reverberated from the hills of Chaplin Creek, telling us that the enemy was at bay. Soon another and another followed in quick succession. We had halted in a long lane at a spring which was dry at the time, when the sound of the first gun reached us. Generals Buell and Mitchell were at the spring, also. They listened attentively for a few moments, then mounted their horses and Buell, addressing a few words to General Mitchell, rode of. General Mitchell placed his division in line of battle on the hills to the right and left of the lane; the 38th was on the hillside to the right. Here we remained all night. We suffered very much for want of water.[3] None could be found for a mile or two in any direction. We explored the neighborhood in every direction without avail. On the morning of the 8th we finally obtained some by sending a detail to a creek about a mile and a half in our front.

On the morning of the 8th, the battle was renewed. The 30th Brigade, belonging to our division, and Captain Hotchkiss with one section of the Minnesota Battery, were ordered forward and got into the engagement to the left of Perryville. About 3 or 4 o'clock P.M. Carlin's Brigade was ordered forward, the 38th being then commanded by Major Gilmer (Colonel O'Kean being absent). We moved forward on the Perryville Road to within about 2 miles of that place, then obliqued to the right through the woods; and after two or three delays emerged into a corn field, passed a battery which was playing on a rebel battery in the woods to the left of the road, and moved forward on double-quick toward Perryville. The field had been previously fought over and the dead and wounded were still on the ground. Hotchkiss' Battery got into position on a hill commanding Perryville and opened fire, and were answered by a rebel battery from a hill beyond the town. The infantry took positions supporting the battery; the 21st on the right, the 38th on the left extending to the Perryville Road.[4]

The firing was kept up by the artillery till dark. In the meantime the skirmish line of the 21st Illinois advanced through the town. At dark the firing ceased for a time, but was renewed by the rebels and kept up briskly for half an hour. It was a splendid sight! The shells flying directly over the town and ricochetting with a lurid glare in the darkness! Just as the moon 'rose, the firing ceased.

Our position was, at this time, on the extreme right of the Union line; nearly a mile, perhaps more, in advance of the other part of the line. A rebel brigade was on the road about half a mile from us, almost in our rear; held in check by the battery we passed in the evening. A few minutes after the shelling ceased, five rebels came down the road from the rebel brigade, going towards the town. Company K, being on the left flank and on the road, quietly made them prisoners. A few minutes later, a rebel surgeon, followed by an ambulance, came down the road and was brought to a sudden halt by an unlooked-for obstruction consisting of a number of Enfield rifles pointing at his breast. Company K then advanced across the road into the woods. Soon after, a rebel caisson (Washington Artillery) came down the road and was intercepted by Company G. After we had remained in the woods about half an hour, having captured several stragglers in the meantime, a rebel ammunition train approached from the town and came within 50 or 60 yards of us. We ordered them to come to us, which they did (thinking us to be rebels), and were only undeceived by finding themselves surrounded by blue uniforms. We captured a total of 13 wagons loaded with ammunition and 68 prisoners; our company numbering only 55 men! We then rejoined the regiment and fell back half a mile and lay by our arms till morning.

The next morning the rebels had again retreated. After the Minnesota Battery having "felt for them" to some extent without effect, we advanced towards the left flank of the Union lines. Crossing the battle grounds of the two preceding days in the Chaplin Creek bottom at about the center of the lines, we passed a great number of arms which appeared to have been grounded and abandoned. We moved to the left across the creek and camped. Here we remained till the 11th. On the night of the 10th, the supply train which had been left at Bowling Green came up with our baggage.

On October 11th we marched towards Harrodsburg. On the evening of the 11th we went into camp about 6 miles from Harrodsburg and put out pickets. We captured four or five rebels at a house near camp. About dark the long roll beat. We fell in and marched in the directions of Danville. We camped about midnight on a creek with General Fry's command. On the 12th we marched in various directions without any apparent purpose, and finally camped in a large open pasture. On the 13th we marched back towards Danville and camped near that place. On the 14th we marched through Danville in the direction of Crab Orchard and overtook the rebel rear guard a few miles from Danville. We skirmished and shelled the woods, advancing slowly, till we arrived at Lancaster at 5 o'clock P.M. We found the rebels in force at Lancaster.

The 2nd Minnesota Battery commenced shelling the town at the distance of about a mile, without eliciting any response. A regiment of cavalry made their appearance on our right flank. Some skirmishing ensued between the rebels and part of the 38th and

General Mitchell's orderlies. The rebels retreated from Lancaster about dark and we went into camp, out of rations.

The train came up next morning about 8 o'clock. We drew rations and marched, another division having gained the advance by our delay. We camped on Dix River, 2 miles from Crab Orchard. We remained at Dix River till the 20th. In the meantime, our baggage train, which we had left the morning of the 7th, came up containing our knapsacks, etc. General Mitchell left us here, leaving General William E. Woodruff in command of the division.

CHAPTER V

Bowling Green to Nashville

"Ol' T Won't Do It.."

The morning of October 20th was cold, and heavy frost lay on the ground when we started towards Lebanon. We camped on a creek, the bridge crossing which the rebels had burnt in their retreat. On the 21st we camped in a field near a creek a few miles south of the Chaplin Hills battleground. On the 22nd we camped on Salt River which is 7 miles from Lebanon. On the twenty-fifth we moved our camp to Rolling Fork. It snowed that night. Having no tents, we made temporary shelters of rails, brush, cornstalks, etc. On the 27th we started for Bowling Green and camped on Pitman's Creek.

We arrived at Bowling Green on November 1st and camped near our former camping ground. On November 4th we marched toward Nashville. We camped at Mitchellville on the 6th and went into camp at Edgefield Junction on the 7th. On the 9th the 38th and the 101st Ohio went to the White Hills and camped at a point where our advance had been attacked by guerrillas on the seventh, preceding. One of the guerrillas had been killed as a result of this attack.

November the 12th we returned to the Junction. On the 13th we moved camp across the road. On Sunday, the 16th, at 2 or 3 o'clock we received orders to march. The 38th Illinois and 15th Wisconsin (in command of Lieutenant Colonel McKee of the 15th Wisconsin) started on a scout to Harpeth Shoals. We camped that evening among the White Hills at a Methodist camp-meeting ground near a large whiskey distillery, which turned out to be the headquarters of the guerrillas of the White Hills. The guerrillas made their appearance within sight of our camp several times.

The next morning we burned the distillery and a house near it and continued our march. The guerrillas were hovering around and watching all our movements, but being careful to keep beyond our reach. We continued our march, slowly, on the Clarksville Road. About 9 or 10 o'clock A.M. we halted and sent a detachment to some houses in the neighborhood which arrested a number of persons, including Major Bradley and two rebel prisoners who had made their escape from Camp Douglas in Chicago.

In the evening a number of men were seen running from a log cabin towards the woods. Companies I and K were sent to look after them and succeeded in capturing old T. Webb, his son, and four others belonging to Peacher's Company of guerrillas. We searched the cabin and found in it arms and U.S. uniforms, etc.. The house was burned by Colonel McKee's orders. It belonged (I believed) to old T's brother who was among the number captured. Old T was laboring under the influence of huge potations of Davidson County whiskey, and was in a gay state of mind. He made strenuous objections to being compelled to walk. He said that Old T "wouldn't walk, couldn't see it." His scruples were overcome, however, by the proximity of U.S. bayonets, and old T was induced to "see it." While we were here a Negro was seen to cross the road and go into the woods on a white horse at full speed. He was brought back, after a short pursuit, in company with another guerrilla. At the next house we captured a sick rebel and took him along in an ambulance. That night we left the Clarksville Road and camped on a road leading to the shoals. On Tuesday, the 18th, it was raining and the road was muddy. We marched at 7 A.M. By 10 o'clock some of our prisoners complained of fatigue. Major Bradley, who is very large and very fat, gave out and we furnished him with a mule, which contrasted admirably with his portly dimensions. Old T was completely sober.

About noon, two Company K boys went to a house some distance from the road to get some water. They told the people that they were Morgan's men (Confederates). The proprietor of the cabin was immensely pleased and gave them their dinner and proposed to go with them to burn out some Union men in the neighborhood. The supposed Morgan men then invited him to come out to the road to see General Morgan, where, to his utter amazement, he found himself taken prisoner (his name was Hutchins).

We camped that evening on Pardue's farm (a Confederate agent) 2 miles from Harpeth Shoals, having captured several prisoners, horses, mules and

arms. Our men destroyed a large quantity of salt
which Pardue had collected for the rebel army.
Colonel McKee, with a mounted squad, went to the
shoals and had a skirmish with some rebels across
the river. On the 19th we started on our return to
camp. On our way back, we camped at Peacher's
Distillery again. That evening we captured a guerrilla
with a horse and double-barreled shot gun in the
woods near camp.

On the 20th we returned to camp via Edgefield,
opposite Nashville. We arrived in camp late in the
night, it having rained every day we were out. On
the 21st we marched to Edgefield and camped on
the railroad on the west side of the road. Here
General Robert B. Mitchell, our former commander,
passed us and was enthusiastically cheered by the
whole command. We remained here till the 28th.
General Jeff C. Davis had arrived at Nashville a few
days before and had taken command of our division.
General Rosencrans [sic] had also arrived about the
seventh and taken command of the Army of the
Cumberland.[5] On the 23rd our division was reviewed
by General Rosencrans [sic] . On the 28th we
moved camp four miles south of Nashville on the
Franklin Pike.

The rebels were in force at Franklin. A slight
skirmish ensued about December 1st between about
seven mounted rebels and our pickets on the Franklin
Pike at a blacksmith shop. A few explosions of the
anvil caused the rebs to retreat in disgust. On
December the 9th we moved to the left seven miles
from Nashville on the Nolensville Pike.

The Army of the Cumberland was reorganized at

Nashville and divided into three corps: 20th Corps on the right, commanded by General A.M. McCook; 14th Corps in the center, commanded by General Thomas; and the 21st Corps on the left, commanded by General Crittenden. The 20th Army Corps was composed of three divisions: Davis' 1st Division; Johnson's 2nd; and Sheridan's 3rd. The 1st Division consisted of three brigades: General Mitchell's 1st; Carlin 2nd; and Woodruff's 3rd.

Nothing of material interest transpired while we remained here, beyond the usual daily routine of camp life. There were reviews, foraging expeditions and drilling activities alternated with occasional picket duty. We stood in line of battle every morning from 4 o'clock till daylight in front of camp. The rebels, under Bragg, were at Murfreesboro, 32 miles from Nashville with outposts at Franklin, Nolensville and Triune. Skirmishing occurred almost daily between the cavalry, foraging parties and pickets of the two armies. On the 24th we received marching orders and marched out two or three miles to our picket lines and then returned to camp. On December 25th orders were given to march at 6 A.M. These orders were then countermanded and we remained in camp.

CHAPTER VI
The Battle of Stones River [6]

DECEMBER, 1862

On December 26th we marched at 7 1/2 A.M. on the Nolensville Pike. It commenced raining soon after we left camp. We met with rebel pickets five miles from Nolensville, and the fighting commenced which resulted in the Battle of Stones River and the evacuation of Murfreesboro by the rebels. [7] We skirmished with the rebel pickets till we arrived at Nolensville, where we were met by a force of rebel cavalry. [8] The 38th formed in skirmish line and advanced to meet them. We attacked them in a grove of cedars on a rocky hill to the right of Nolensville, and drove them from their positions. [61] We then marched on towards Triune and found the rebels in force at Knob Gap, two miles from Nolensville. Their force consisted of a brigade of dismounted cavalry and a battery of 58 pieces. Their battery opened up on us at a distance of about one mile and a half. Hotchkiss' battery unlimbered and returned the compliment. Carlin's brigade was ordered to charge the rebel battery, which we did, crossing an open and very muddy cornfield. We were exposed for a distance of a mile to their fire, which was concentrated on the left of the 38th; Companies H, I, and K suffering the most severely. Soon after we commenced our advance, G.W. Stockwell of our company was wounded by a shell. Soon after that, A. P. Berlin was struck down in the same manner. Next, John G. Bliss was wounded in the leg by a fragment of a shell. The rebel battery played upon us in full blast, and our own battery in our rear (in the ineffectual attempt to cover our advance) exposed us to still more danger by their own shells bursting prematurely over our heads.

The air resounded with the hideous noise of the shells, whizzing and bursting; before us, behind us, above us and among us. As soon as we got within range, they opened up on us with musketry. About this time Minor Mitchell of Company K fell, pierced through the breast with a piece of shell. He died about three hours afterward. When we got within about 150 yards of them, we gave them a volley. They soon after retreated, leaving one piece of artillery in our possession. We captured seven prisoners, including one that had been captured in the skirmish with the cavalry at Nolensville.

A gang of cattle got between the lines during the fight and ran wildly from line to line. One of them had its leg broken by a rebel shell and was devoured by the heroes of the day. We camped that night on the field of battle. The rebs did not disturb us, but an unfortunate horse, having approached the picket lines without the proper countersign, was killed wises of those who now so eagerly marched across it. When we moved into the woods, we were arranged in the order of battle. The 38th and the 101st Ohio were held in reserve; the 21st Illinois and 15th Wisconsin moved forward and attacked the rebels, who were stationed behind a fence across a small field. The fighting was severe. The rebel grape and canister rapidly thinned our ranks. Our men were repeatedly driving back, but only to advance with renewed determination. The Norwegians fought like tigers and held their ground with Scandinavian tenacity, though often wavering before the deadly fire. Colonel Alexander of the 21st charged with his regiment on the rebel battery, but was driven back with a loss of nearly half his men. Darkness put an end to the fight with heavy loss on both sides, and we lay down by our arms to sleep; "the weary to rest and the wounded to die." We were in a low flat cedar woods, or grove. The rebels were 100 to 200 yards in front of us. The night was very cold. About 8 or 10 o'clock ses of those who now so eagerly marched across it. When we moved into the woods, we were arranged in the order of battle. The 38th and the 101st Ohio were held in reserve; the 21st Illinois and 15th Wisconsin moved forward and attacked the rebels, who were stationed behind a fence across a small field. The fighting was severe. The rebel grape and canister rapidly thinned our ranks. Our men were repeatedly driving back, but only to advance with renewed determination. The Norwegians fought like tigers and held their ground with Scandinavian tenacity, though often wavering before the deadly fire. Colonel Alexander of the 21st charged with his regiment on the rebel battery, but was driven back with a loss of nearly half his men. Darkness put an end to the fight with heavy loss on both sides, and we lay down by our arms to sleep; "the weary to rest and the wounded to die." We were in a low flat cedar woods, or grove. The rebels were 100 to 200 yards in front of us. The night was very cold. About 8 or 10 o'clock a sharp volley was heard from our line of sentinels, which was occasioned by some movement among the rebels. In a few moments the firing subsided and "all was quiet on Stones River" till morning, and we once more closed our eyes on the events of the day while we "bitterly thought of the morrow."

The morning of December 31st dawned clear and cold. The rebels had employed the night in massing their forces on the right wing of our army, which was commanded by General McCook. At daylight they renewed the battle by attacking General Johnson's division on our extreme right. Being taken by surprise, they were soon driven back in confusion. The rebels then closed upon our lines from the right towards the left, attacking brigade after brigade in overwhelming numbers and driving them back with immense loss. The rapid volleys of musketry mingled with the roar of artillery, the screeching and bursting shells reverberated through the dark cedar forest. Each volley sounding "nearer, clearer, and deadlier than before," informed us that the tide of battle was rolling toward us and would soon be upon us at last. When the sun had gotten about an hour high, and was shining down red, cold and cheerless, the rebel horde appeared in our front. Johnson's division was in full retreat, the rebel cavalry was swarming 'round upon our rear. Masses of rebels in front of us kept up a terrific fire. Our ranks were being rapidly thinned. Woodruff's brigade, on our left were repeatedly driven back and repeatedly rallied and recovered their ground. The unbroken lines of rebels advanced slowly and steadily upon us. At last, Woodruff's brigade broke their ranks and retreated in confusion, our left being thus uncovered. The rebels were rapidly outflanking us. A sharp volley from our left checked them momentarily, and their most exposed ranks fell back. They had, however, turned our right, and we were ordered to retreat. A few minutes longer stay would have resulted in the capture of the whole brigade.

We fell back leaving Captain Mead of Company F and Lieutenant Dillon killed, Lieutenant Scott of Company K mortally wounded, besides numbers of our men. Lieutenant Colonel McKee of the 15th Wisconsin had expressed a wish that if he were killed in battle that he might be shot in the temple, was left dead upon the field, shot in the temple. We retreated across that memorable Cotton field, the rebels firing at us with deadly effect; the rebel cavalry were drawn up to charge on us, but were restrained from some cause.

In the opposite woods we rallied and the 2nd Minnesota Battery returned the rebel's fire, but the rebel shot and grape (which they gave us without stint) were arguments too persuasive to be disregarded, and we again retreated. Colonel Heg of the 15th Wisconsin and Lieutenant Colonel Gilmer commanding the 38th (Colonel O'Kean having resigned at Rolling Fork) united the remnants of their regiments and made a stand about a mile and a half from the first line of battle, behind a fence where the rebels would be exposed in crossing a field. We were unable to check them and retreated, leaving two of our company wounded, Lee and Christian. Dire confusion now became the order of the day. Infantry, artillery, army wagons and mules were mixed up in one wild retreat.[9]

Near the railroad we passed General Rosencrans [sic] , leading a charge of Rousseau's division, which turned the scale in our favor. We rallied at the railroad and finally, after marching in several directions and meeting with one or two threatened encounters, took our station on the extreme right to the right of the railroad. Our regiment now numbered about 190; Company K numbered 27 men (a great many of them missing) had gotten lost from their command in the retreat. Company K's losses were: Lieutenant Scott and T.A. Reed, wounded mortally; Lee McDowell, Burnside and A. Hankins, wounded; Henry C. Moore, Powell, Chaplain I.P. Reed, E. Reisner and B.M. Bridges, prisoners; and Brackett and English missing or deserted.

About dark a fight occurred between two cavalry regiments near our position. The Union cavalry drove the rebels past our right and into the opposite woods, part of a large plantation separating us from the rebels.

The next morning was January 1st, 1863 and companies were detailed from the different regiments for picket. Company K was detailed from the 38th. We formed a skirmish line in a grove 100 yards in front of the brigade, and proceeded to erect breastworks of rails. About eight or nine o'clock the rebels commenced shelling our position and were replied to by Hotchkiss' battery. A large eagle had coolly taken his position on the tallest tree in the grove over our heads, and quietly maintained that position in spite of shot and shell. About noon a rebel brigade advanced to attack us. They were protected by a deep ravine till they got within 150 yards of us. Then we opened fire on them and two shells from the "Chicago Board of Trade,"[10] (the last one dropping right into their ranks, killing ten of them as they said) caused them to retreat in the utmost confusion. Two-hundred of them (including Lieutenant Lidell, brother of the General) surrendered on the spot. Nothing more occurred that day.[11]

On January 2nd, in the evening, Breckenridge's division made an attack on the center, but was driven back with immense loss. The rebels then attacked the left on the other side of the river. At 4 P.M. Davis' division was ordered to the left, we went on double quick and crossed Stones River just as the fighting ceased. We lay in line till 1 o'clock A.M., then commenced building breastworks of rails and mud. On the 3rd we were kept on the alert by rebel sharpshooters who kept up a constant fire on us from a strip of woods opposite or position. Just after dark the rebels made an attack on the lines on our right, and, after an hour or two of hard fighting they again fell back. And so ended the Battle of Stones River, for the rebels evacuated Murfreesboro that night.

On January 4th we recrossed Stones River at 2 A.M. and camped near the railroad about four miles from Murfreesboro. On the 5th a detail was made to bury the dead. Before the battle our regiment numbered 650. It now numbered 318.[12] On the 5th and 6th we moved camp two miles south of Murfreesboro on the right of the Shelbyville Pike.

Bragg retreated to Shelbyville and Tullohoma. On the 11th the 38th went to Nashville guarding a supply train, returned on the 13th. On the 31st Davis' division started to Franklin. We camped that evening at Eagleville with one or two other divisions.

CHAPTER VII

Skirmishing in Tennessee

FEBRUARY, 1863

On February the 1st we camped seven miles from Franklin. On February 2nd we arrived at Franklin on Big Harpeth River. We marched through the town and camped a half mile by and on the Columbia Road. The 38th Regiment was on picket that night. On the 4th our company was detailed for Provost Guard in Franklin and quartered in the court house. General Davis took the cavalry of the expedition and went on a scout leaving the infantry at Franklin. He captured several prisoners as a result of the expedition and was joined by several refugees. On the 12th we started on our return to camp. Marched to Eagleville. [11] Two houses were burnt in Eagleville that night. Origin of the fires was unknown. We arrived at camp at 2 P.M. on the 13th. March 4th the train of General Johnson's division went on a foraging excursion on the Salem Pike. Carlin's brigade, commanded by Colonel Heg of the Norwegian regiment, marched at daylight to protect them. Turning to the left of the pike four miles from camp, we encountered a squad of rebel cavalry which retreated.

Continuing our march, we met several squads of rebels numbering from five to thirty or forty. Company K, being in advance as skirmishers, exchanged a few shots with them. We then turned to the left and marched to the Shelbyville Pike, which is nine miles from Murfreesboro. About 2 P.M. we reached the pike between the rebel outpost and their sentinels. We captured the two sentinels quietly and our company advanced on double-quick towards the outpost station, the smoke from their fire being visible behind the next hills. We got within twenty or thirty yards unobserved, then halted and fired and charged upon them. They were sitting and lying around their fire, their horses tied to the cedars and their arms scattered about. About that time of day there commenced a scene of dire confusion among the Johnnies. Some sprung upon their horses and spurred vigorously, forgetting to untie before mounting. Then springing off, they plunged wildly down the hillside which was covered with cedars; others executed a series of prodigious jumps down the steep hillside and disappeared in the cedar thicket. The result of our charge was one prisoner, one horse killed, about a dozen horses captured, 10 or 12 Springfield muskets, a few carbines, cartridge boxes, saddles, bridles, U.S. and C.S. blankets, quilts, jeans, hats, an old pair of gloves and 1 pocket knife, etc. We then returned to camp with the spoils.

On March 6th, the brigade again marched out to the same place, found the rebels in force. The artillery and infantry skirmished all day; losses on our side were slight. Next morning at 3 o'clock, we returned to camp. On the 9th, the division marched on the Salem Pike and camped at Versailles. On the

10th we marched towards Triune. Our brigade encountered Steadman's pickets four miles from Triune. A skirmish ensued between our advance and the pickets; each taking the other for rebels. We drove them back toward Triune, where General Steadman's forces were. We captured two or three of them, and sent them to inform the others of their mistake. We camped late at night about a mile from Triune. On the 13th we returned to Eaglesville, the 14th to Versailles, and the 15th we were at camp.

On March 18th the division was placed on the Salem outpost, 38th on picket, Major H. N. Alden in command. At 3 o'clock A.M. a detachment of 12 of our company, one company of the 15th Wisconsin, and 5 or 6 cavalrymen were sent out to surprise a rebel picket post which our spy had discovered in the evening previous. The Norwegians went round to get in the rear. Volunteers were called for to go in advance and find the rebels, the cavalry following, ready to charge as soon as we found them. Three of us volunteered for that duty and moved towards the rebels. The night was very dark. We moved down the road about half a mile and met the Norwegians returning, the rebels having fallen back in the early part of the night. A fight came very near taking place between the Norwegians and ourselves, but we fortunately discovered the state of things in time to prevent it.

On March 21st the rebels attacked the Union lines in our rear, skirmishing all day. On the 22nd we were relieved and returned to the lines. We moved camp one mile from Murfreesboro to the west of the Shelbyville Pike. The Union forces were now drawn in around Murfreesboro and camped more compactly, and fortifications were commenced.

On April 4th our regiment worked on the fortifications and on the railroad. On the 15th the 2nd Brigade went again on the outpost near Salem between Murfreesboro and Salem, left of the pike. We were relieved on the 20th and returned to camp.

In May, water being the article we now most desired, wells were commenced in nearly every regiment; but unfortunately for us we invariably found a bed of rock from 5 to 8 feet below the surface. Blasting was resorted to and continued for a considerable time without penetrating through the rocky bed in a single instance. On the 14th our brigade went on outpost at Manchester Heights four miles south of Murfreesboro. On the 16th the rebels with artillery attacked our position, skirmishing all day. In the evening the 38th was sent round to the right to outflank them, but the Johnnies, thinking discretion the better part of valor, limbered to the rear on quick-time. The next morning we were relieved by the 3rd Brigade which was commanded by Colonel Hans C. Heg. On the night of the 24th, Clement L. Vallandigham (the "Great Banished") passed our camp en route for rebeldom.[13]

On the 28th we went on outpost again at Manchester Heights. We camped on Stones River, left of the railroad, or rather on the railroad. Skirmishing was kept up on June 4th. The 38th was held in reserve. On June 7th we were relieved and returned to camp. On June 24th our army left Murfreesboro. Davis' and Johnson's divisions marched toward Liberty Gap. It rained that night. On the 25th we marched to the gap, halted at the camp from which Johnson had driven the rebels the day before. In the afternoon, Willich's brigade (of the 2nd Division) attacked the rebel General Lidell's brigade of Claiborne's division, which was stationed on a high hill commanding the valley. Hard fighting ensued. Willich's brigade, or the regiments of it (77th Pennsylvania and 79th, 34th and 30th Illinois), gained the foot of the hill and sheltered themselves behind a fence on the bank of a creek which ran around the foot of the hill. At 4 o'clock P.M. we were ordered to the advance. Willich's men ran out of ammunition and the 38th was ordered forward to their support. We went forward double-quick, passed through an orchard and into a very muddy field of young corn. The rebel battery opened on us, and as soon as we got in range the rebels on the hill commenced on us. Willich's men, being out of ammunition, retreated in disorder. The rebels, with fixed bayonets, advanced to the foot of the hill and prepared to charge. Willich's men, when we met them, laid down and we passed over them and opened a sharp fire on the advancing rebs, which quickly sent them back to the top of the hill. They again opened on us with renewed energy and the hillside was enveloped in a cloud of smoke. We quickly crossed the cornfield and road, waded the creek, and closed up to the fence, and not a live reb was then to be seen. A line of skirmishers was sent to the top of the hill and there found about 30 killed and 1 or 2 wounded and took them prisoner. The battle flag of the 2nd Arkansas was found, the color sergeant laying across it on his face, dead; his hands grasping the staff of the "Bonny Blue Flag," the color guard all killed. We lay at the foot of the hill that night, our picket on the top of the hill.

The next morning, June 26th, the rebels were discovered on the next hill, a wheat field filling the narrow valley between us. Regiments of rebels were seen marching to our right along a chain of hills on which the rebel line was posted. Our company was sent forward as skirmishers across the valley. We marched across the field and almost to the fence at the foot of the hill to which our men wished to advance. We then halted and laid down about twenty yards from the fence. About that time a rebel brigade, which had been concealed at the top of this hill opened a deadly fire upon us. Major Alden, being in command of the skirmish line, gave the command "Advance, double-quick!" We rose to our feet, and the Major, perhaps receiving a gentle but persuasive hint from the whistle of a rebel minnie ball in disagreeable proximity to his cranium, quickly changed his command to "Skirmishers in retreat!" which we obeyed with alacrity, giving the rebs a farewell token.

Eventually, as we retreated, we regained the fence on our own side of the valley and opened on the rebels who now quietly subsided. Then Companies A and B were ordered forward in skirmish line. Old Jimmy Hemphill of Company A, declaring himself unable to comprehend, "What Could Major Alden mean, to take us down there and hang us on the mercy of God! Sure, if Company K could'n whip the bloody spalpanes, it's no use for A and B to try!" They advanced nearly to the fence, then the rebels opened on them. They advanced on the run to the fence, but were soon forced to retreat. This ended the active fighting for the day. Skirmishing was kept up all day, however.

CHAPTER VIII
Talkin' to Johnnie Reb

JUNE, 1863

With each party remaining concealed on his own side of the fence, being within conversing distance, a conversation was kept up between the Yanks and Johnnies. These were the men we had fought at the river, consequently we were old acquaintances. The Johnnies sent such questions as "How far have you advanced today, Yank?" "What do you think of Chancellorsville?" "Where's General Hooker?" "Come over Yank and get your rations!" "Come over and get your knapsacks!" and "Here's your Lager beer, bring on your Dutchman (referring to Rosencrans [sic])" And our men returned them such as "How do you like Valladingham?" "Come over and get your flag," etc. The next morning no rebels were to be seen. The 101st Ohio were sent out in skirmish line. They went about a mile in our front and found nary reb. We then marched to the left through Hoover's Gap and camped at Beech Grove. On the 28th we marched toward Manchester, and camped on Duck River, one mile from Manchester.

On July 1st we marched to Tullahoma and camped southwest of the town; it having been evacuated by the rebels the day before. On July 2nd we marched to Elk River. A skirmish took place at the ford between our advance and the rebels. We went up the river and camped. On the 3rd we resumed our march. It was raining. We waded Elk River which was waist deep and rapid. We captured some rebel stragglers near Winchester. We waded Boaring Fork, which was deeper and more rapid than Elk River, and camped in Winchester. On the 4th of July a salute was fired by the 2nd Minnesota Battery. On the 7th, an official dispatch of the surrender of Vicksburg and the defeat of Lee at Gettysburg was received At Winchester. On the 9th we moved camp to the west of town. On the 11th, the pickets being changed left us outside of the lines. We accordingly moved camp further to the left and within the lines. On this day the cars also commenced running to Winchester. Previous to this our rations were hauled from Elk River. Numbers of citizens drew rations from the commissary. Consequently, the soldiers' rations were growing smaller by degrees and beautifully less. They now soon began to grow more abundant in quantity, though sadly deficient in quality.

It was now August 6th, Thanksgiving Day. A meeting was held in Davis' division which was attended by Generals Garfield, McCook and Davis. On August 17th a forward movement commenced. We marched at 2 P.M., having remained at Winchester since July 3rd. The day was extremely warm, forcing us to march very slowly. A great many of us were overcome by the heat, and lined the roadside for miles. We went into camp on a farm at the foot of the Cumberland Mountains, having marched six miles, which sufficed to fill the division ambulances with men who had given out from the effects of the heat. On the 18th we climbed the Cumberland Mountains and camped on top of the mountain to the left of the road about one-half mile out in the wild woods. On the 19th we descended the mountain and camped in a beautiful little valley at the foot of the mountains on a creek. Roasting ears and peaches were abundant in this valley and we went for them pretty extensively. As we were descending the mountain, General Carlin's orderly, Joe, was shot by a guerrilla and severely wounded.

On the next day, August 20th, we marched to Stevenson which was seven miles distant. We camped on the railroad west of Stevenson (about a mile or a mile and a half) at a steam saw mill, where the Pioneer Brigade of Sheridan's division was camped. We arrived here about noon. Here, as on many other occasions, we were camped about a mile from water, which we had to carry from a large spring, or sink hole, at a creek one mile distant. The country about Stevenson was filled with small squads of guerrillas, roving over the country and hanging all the soldiers they could catch for amusement; and getting hung themselves when caught. Our first duty here was to clean off a drill/parade ground with immense labor; Colonel Gilmer having selected the brushiest spot he could find in the extremely brushy wilderness "way down in Alabam." Picket duty and foraging were our recreations. Peaches, melons, sweet potatoes, poultry, and other fruit were abundant.

On the 29th of this month, we marched to Caperton's Ferry on the Tennessee River about three miles distant. We camped in a grove near the river in an old field grown over with briers and apricot vines. This evening our Chaplain held divine services in the grove. The evening of the 29th and the morning of the 30th was occupied by the Pioneer Brigade in placing a pontoon bridge across the river. On the evening of the 30th we crossed the river on the pontoon bridge and camped with Colonel Brownlow's East Tennessee Cavalry in the river bottom. On the 31st we climbed the Sand Mountains and camped on their top on a small stream in a beautiful level, open woods.

We remained here till September 2nd when we marched to the foot of the mountain and camped, having marched fifteen miles. In crossing these mountains we were joined by a great many men who had been hid among the mountains to avoid the rebel conscription, and a few deserters from the rebel army. On the 3rd a squad from the 38th went out toward Wills Valley on a foraging excursion. Two miles from camp we were informed that rebels were in the neighborhood. There were about 20 of us. We pursued them to the valley head. At that place we overtook one, a Dr. somebody, and a malignant rebel. We then started on our return. We arrived at camp about 1 P.M., and found the brigade preparing to march. We marched at half past one P.M. one mile back toward the mountain and camped on the mountain side near a little farm, the owner of which had some time previously been shot in his cornfield by rebels.

On the 4th we marched at 2 o'clock P.M. for four more miles and camped at Valley Head Post Office at the head of Lookout and Will's Valleys which run into each other here. We got into camp about 10

P.M. We camped in Will's Valley at the foot of Lookout Mountain. Water was abundant and good forage rather scarce. Rations were nearly "played out." We remained here till the 9th. While in camp here a squad from our brigade went on a foraging excursion to the top of Lookout Mountain. They were surprised in a peach orchard on the mountain by guerrillas. One or two were killed, some taken prisoner, and a few escaped. The prisoners were afterward found dead in the woods near the creek on which they were captured, having been murdered by the guerrillas.

On the 9th we marched at 8 A.M. and crossed Lookout Mountain, marching southeast. Camped at the foot of the mountain in Broomtown Valley near the Georgia line, the right of the road in a field. On the 10th our brigade went into camp in a grove to the left of the road about 200 yards. This is a beautiful valley. There is forage in abundance, corn, etc. On the 13th we marched back to the top of the mountain and camped. There was no water near camp. On the 14th we marched towards Valley Head and halted on the creek on top of the mountain where our boys were killed by the guerrillas a few days before. We remained about one hour, then marched on past Valley Head and camped in Lookout Valley to the left of the Lebanon Road, 20 miles from Lebanon and 4 miles from Valley Head. That night we received a large mail, the first we had received since the 9th.

On the 15th, at 4 1/2 P.M. we marched to Valley Head, and drew rations. We received hard-tack half rations, pickled pork; two days' worth for nine. On the 16th we marched onto Lookout Mountain, turned to the left, crossed the mountain, and camped on the mountainside near its foot in a small narrow valley. On the 17th we descended the mountain into McLemore's Cove. We halted on a large creek about an hour; then marched, passed some breastworks which some of our men had thrown up where a fight had occurred the day before, and went into camp (or rather formed in line of battle) in front of Dug Gap, where the rebels were supposed to be.

On the 18th we drew rations and moved in the late evening towards Chattanooga three miles and camped; moving after dark to prevent our movements from being discovered by the rebels. We camped that night in a field near a large creek.

CHAPTER IX

The Battle of Chickamauga

SEPTEMBER, 1863

On September 19th the Battle of Chickamauga commenced between the Army of the Cumberland under General William S. Rosencrans and the rebels under Bragg, reinforced by Longstreet's division from Virginia. McCook's Corps was camped 18 miles from Chattanooga. We commenced our march toward Chattanooga about 7 or 8 o'clock A.M. Sheridan's division was in front, Johnson's next and Davis' last. Soon after we commenced our march, the firing of artillery two or three miles in front of us broke upon our ears. Soon cavalry or infantry were heard skirmishing a few hundred yards on our right flank; but McCook "cared for none of these things." We kept on our march rapidly, without halting for an instant.[14] Next we passed a battery on the right of the road that was in position for action, while rifle skirmishing was going on briskly a short distance further out in the woods. After we passed the battery, we passed a house to the left of the road,

59 • William Elwood Patterson

where we passed General McCook, with his corps flag and orderlies.

We then emerged into an open field with thick woods to the right of the road where sharp skirmishing was going on. Near the road as we were passing through this open space, one of our regiment was wounded by a rebel ball from the woods. We halted here a few moments, then moved forward again on the Chattanooga Road. We halted at Crawfish Spring about an hour, it being about noon when we arrived at the spring. We moved again about 1 o'clock. We heard no more of the skirmishing to the right of the road, but could see the dust raised by the rebel column about a mile to our right. On the forward move towards Chattanooga, about a mile from the springs, we passed another battery to our right (in position), and could hear severe artillery and rifle firing in our front.

Then we knew that another battle had commenced and we hoped before night to crush Bragg and the rebel army out of existence and finish the rebellion in the west; while the rebels were equally certain that the opportunity had arrived when they might expel the invader from the sacred soil, and drive the "Vandals" back to their "Northern Hives." We passed large gangs of Negroes, laying by the roadsides in the hot sun, fast asleep. They belonged to the army, and when the battle commenced they remained in the rear and improved the time by their favorite recreation, sleeping.

As we approached nearer to the field of battle, the firing seemed to increase and soon became terrific, volley after volley, broken by continual and incessant peals of artillery resounding through the woods and over the fields of Chickamauga. We passed a large farm near the battlefield, the fence of which had been set on fire and the rails were now burning and smoking in the ashes. A few hundred yards further we arrived at the scene of action on the banks of Chickamauga Creek, 10 miles from Chattanooga and 3 miles from Crawfish Spring. Chickamauga Creek was on the right side of the road as we approached Chattanooga and the rebels were on the creek. [11]

The battle commenced on the left of the line towards Chattanooga, both armies being in line of march from below towards Chattanooga. The heads of the columns had come in collision about 10 miles from Chattanooga and closed on each other from left to right like the blades of a pair of scissors. As we approached the field of battle the 2nd Minnesota Battery (belonging to our brigade) dashed off through the woods to the right, got into position and opened on the rebels.

The infantry kept on a short distance and filed to the right and took a position about 200 yards to the right of the road at about 2? P.M. The firing was tremendous. No rattling fire, but volley after volley, without intermission as fresh regiments were forming in line every minute. Far, far to the left (away towards Chattanooga and all along down the line to our own brigade) were heard the incessant and terrific volleys of musketry, the unbroken thunder of artillery, the shells screeching and bursting, tearing off the tops and branches of trees or lacerating human ranks. The cheers of Union or rebel soldiers resounded as each, by turn, gained a transient advantage. Such firing I have never heard before or since.

Our brigade formed in line on the right of the Union line of battle. The 3rd Brigade was commanded by Colonel Hans C. Heg of the 15th Wisconsin; which regiment had been transferred to the 3rd Brigade at Murfreesboro. The 81st Indiana (being transferred to the 2nd) was on the left wing of the division. The 2nd Brigade was on the right. The 1st Brigade, commanded by Mitchell, was at Nashville on post duty. Our division formed in line and were ordered to lay down. Colonel Heg, with part of his brigade, advanced rapidly into the woods and were fired on by the rebels. They opened a sharp fire and continued to move forward, rapidly driving the rebels before them and soon disappeared into the woods. The firing then became heavier. Soon our men were seen retreating in confusion, the rebels following them closely with a destructive fire; killing and wounding a great many of them. Our men fell back to our position, rallied and formed in line on our left. We opened fire on the advancing rebels and held them in check. Then Colonel Heg again advanced with his men, reinforced by the 21st Illinois. They again drove the rebels before them as before, and disappeared into the woods under a heavy fire.

During all this time, our brigade remained in line, laying down, and at this time were only exposed to the rebel artillery and straggling shots from the rebel lines. After a short but severe fight in the woods in front of us, Heg's men were again seen retreating in complete disorder, the rebels pressing them closely. They fell back to our lines and were formed in line again on our left. We immediately opened fire on the advancing rebels, but were unable to check them. They continued to advance slowly, concealing themselves behind the trees and keeping up a destructive fire upon us. The rebel artillery then became quite annoying. A ball from a rebel cannon tore a large limb from a tree a few feet in front of us and it fell almost in our ranks.

Our company was very much exposed, being out in an old road or open space in full view of the rebels, who had the advantage of the trees in the thick woods. The rebels continued to advance slowly till they were within 100 yards of us. The minnie and musket balls began to fall among us thick and fast with deadly effect. I.P. Moulden was first wounded in the thigh, then Rotzler, next Christian in the shoulder, then Eli K. Dowell through the bowels. The rebels were now within 60 or 70 yards of us. Every tree and log concealed a rebel. Their balls fell among us like hail, one after another was shot down in rapid succession. Their fire still grew fiercer and more deadly. One after another of us felt the sudden stunning shock as we were struck by the rebel bullet, depriving us for a moment almost of sensation. Then the blood upon our clothes, making us aware that we were wounded. (I was wounded at this time).

At this time we had been in the fight apparently not longer than 20 minutes, it might have been an hour. After maintaining their position for some time under this deadly fire and with heavy loss of killed and wounded, Davis' division fell back across the road, where they remained the night of the 19th, having sustained almost incredible loss of killed and wounded. After dark on the 19th, the musicians of the 38th went onto the field to relieve the wounded, and were fired upon by the rebels and J. Murray of Company I was killed. On the morning of the 20th of September, the rebels renewed the battle. Davis' division advanced, was attacked and their left flank turned, swinging their line around like a door. They retreated and again rallied behind some breastworks that had been thrown up some time previously. The rebels again advanced upon the, and were about to surround them, and they again retreated, the 38th leaving their fearless Colonel Daniel Gilmer dead on the field. They then retreated towards Chattanooga, the "Ne plus ultra" to the rebels. They camped, or rather, slept on their arms about 6 miles from Chattanooga at Rossville, and on the 22nd what was left of them marched weary and dejected (though not despondent) into Chattanooga.[15]

Colonel Heg of the 15th Wisconsin, J.W.S. Alexander of the 21st Illinois, and Gilmer of the 38th were killed in this battle. Major H.N. Alden, Captain Wells of the 38th wounded, Captain Cole mortally. The men of Company K, 38th Illinois who were killed were: David B. Hankins, E.H. Dowell. Those wounded were: Jonathan Foster, Martin Christian (both died of their wounds), J.P. Moulden, Rotzler, John W. Brooks, B.M. Bridges, Jonathan Trexler, William Worthy, and William E. Patterson. Those taken prisoner were: Joe Allison, David Bowers, J. Chesnut, J.D. Devine, J. Francis, M.H. Bridges, Ithamar Clark, Henry C. Moore, Joe Shedelbauer, William Sutton, and John R. Malcolm.

CHAPTER X

Wounded, Captured, Paroled, Home

SEPTEMBER, 1863

I was wounded at Chickamauga on September 19, 1863 at about 3 o'clock P.M. The ball was extracted by the surgeon of the 65th Illinois Regiment. I was sent to Davis' Division Hospital at Crawfish Spring. The hospital was at Gordon's house. On the evening of the 20th all the wounded who could bear transportation were sent to Chattanooga in a train of ambulances and army wagons. Soon after they left, the 11th Regiment of Texas Rangers made their appearance and captured the hospital, making us all prisoners. We were kept here as prisoners of war for ten days. Our diet was mush twice a day. Some who were able to walk were started towards Richmond, Virginia. On the 29th they commenced paroling the wounded prisoners here and sent part of them through the lines to Chattanooga on a train of ambulances which General Rosencrans had sent through the lines for us.

On September the 30th the rest of us were paroled

and on October 1st we started through the lines for Chattanooga. We were paroled by Captain Reed C.S., a quartermaster of the rebel army. About dark the ambulances corralled in a field to the left of the road, and the rebel drivers went off to their camp leaving us to our fate. On the morning of the 2nd we passed the lines and arrived at Chattanooga and were placed in hospitals. When paroled we were sworn not to serve in any capacity or any branch of the service of the United States until exchanged and not to reveal anything detrimental to the interests of the Confederate States. On the evening of the 2nd at dark, we were sent from Chattanooga to the field hospital across the river. We met teamsters retreating from Sequatchie Valley, where they had been attacked by rebels. Our ambulances arrived at the hospital very late that night.

On October 4th the wounded men started to Stevenson, Alabama in a supply train. Rations being scarce, we were supplied with two crackers apiece for the trip. We stopped that night on the bank of the Tennessee River at the foot of the mountain. On October 5th, we commenced ascending the mountain. The starved mules were hardly able to climb the mountain without the wagons. We got half way up the mountain against dark and stopped the wagons which stood in the road till morning. On the 6th we were able to get to the top of the mountain into Sequatchie Valley where we met a forage train with some corn. Our two crackers having disappeared, we got a supply of corn in the husk. We camped that night at Jasper and got some rations. On the 7th we arrived at Stevenson. We left Stevenson on the 11th and boarded a freight train, arriving in Tullahoma at

2 A.M. Then, on to Murfreesboro and finally Nashville at 11 A. M.

I was admitted to Hospital No. 1, at 2nd Division, Major Cyrus Horner in charge. I was assigned to Ward No. 6, Surgeon A. McDill in charge. On December 1st I was transferred to Ward No. 2 (upstairs) in the old cannon foundry. January 1st was extremely cold, the 14th was transferred to Ward No 1. (upstairs) On February 10th I was transferred to Louisville and admitted to Brown General Hospital, No 7, Ward No 4, and later transferred, on the 12th, to Ward No 1.

On the 14th I was assigned to Invalid Corps, 2nd Battalion and sent to Jefferson Hospital at Jeffersonville. On the 16th I applied to Provost Marshall General E. M. Goodwin at Nashville for certificatte of parole. On February 29th I left the 44th Company, 2nd Battalion V>R>C>, went to barracks in Jeffersonville to go to Camp Chase, Ohio. On March the 1st, I was sent to exchange barracks in Louisville. On the 2nd I started to Camp Chase. March 3rd arrived at Camp Chase at 7 A.M. May the 2nd started home on furlough. Arrived home May 3rd 1864. On May 6th, at 8 A.M. I arrived at Nashville and stayed at the Tollicoffer House. I left there at 12 noon on Tuesday the 7th and arrived at Stevenson, Alabama at 1 A.M. the next day. Exchanged May 7th. On Thursday evening, the 9th, I started towards Chattanooga, arriving there on the 10th (via Bridgeport). Started back May 31st. Arrived back at Camp Chase on June 1st. June 2nd, Started to Dixie. The 3rd at Lydel Barracks, Cincinnati. Sunday the 5th at Louisville,

I was then sent to Camp of Detachments, 2nd Battalion, 10th Street, 4th Corps. Major Peloubet Commanding Camps, Major Hanna Commanding 2nd Battalion. The 38th Illinois detachment arrived at Chattanooga on September 13th, to be mustered out, the regiment having reenlisted. The detachment numbered 80 or 90 or about that number. On September 15th we were mustered out of the United States service. On the 16th, we started home again, via Nashville and Louisville. On the 19th we were paid off.

September 20th found us at Olney, Illinois. On September 21st, 1864 arrived at Home. Those of Company K returning home were William M. Babbs, G. M. Brooks, B. M. Bridges, H. L. Bliss, Frank Carter, William Dillman, Ezra Cather, N[athan] Cather, Robert Ping, Napoleon Bonaparte Parker, Sam Scott, Jonathan Trexler, William and E. Worthy, Michael Stockwell, Eliphaz Reisner, and B. W. Harris.

W. E. Patterson

William E. Patterson (circa 1910)

CHAPTER XI

Footnotes

1 By early April, Grant had his men at Pittsburg Landing (also referred to as "Shiloh"). Buell's men had not yet arrived, but they were on their way. Pittsburg Landing was a small riverboat settlement. It was a few miles from the country meeting house known as Shiloh Church, a little more than twenty miles from the main Confederate force at Corinth. *The Golden Book of the Civil War*, (Golden Press, New York, 1960), 43.

2 Perryville was the site of the major battle of the Kentucky campaign on October 8, 1862 and is located about ten miles due west of Danville. Robert U. Johnson and Clarence C. Buel (eds.), *Battles and Leaders of the Civil War* (4 vols.; New York, 1956), III, 30.

3 The Union Army that advanced toward this position on October 7 was desperately short of water. One captain recalled having "but one cracker" and no water on the hot, sixteen mile march from Spring-field. Another Union soldier later remembered "here

and there a stagnant pool from which the exhausted soldiers would sweep off the thick scum and dipped [sic] up the nauseous liquid to moisten their parched lips." The streams and pools around Perryville offered their first real hope of fresh water. Dr. Kenneth A. Hafendorfer, Perryville, *Battle for Kentucky*, (Louisville), #8.

4   At 12:00 Noon, October 8, 1862, the Confederate line ran roughly north and south. In the area were men of the 16th and 33rd Alabama, 3rd Confederate an 45th Mississippi infantry regiments as well as the 15th Battalion of Mississippi Sharpshooters and Semples' Alabama Battery. These units made up S.A.M. Wood's Brigade. Also present was F.J. Jones' Brigade composed of the 27th, 30th and 37th Mississippi infantry regiments and Lumsden's Alabama Battery. Other units, mainly under the command of Kentuckian Simon Bolivar Buckner, deployed further along the line. These men crossed the Chaplin River from Harrodsburg Pike earlier in the morning. They continued westward and attacked Alexander McCooks' Union First Army Corps. Some fought their way over a mile in that direction and approached the intersection of Hayes-Mayes and White's Road by 6:00 P. M. After Union forces stopped the Confederate advance in that area, many of the Confederates fell back. It was the beginning of a retreat that would eventually carry them all the way out of Kentucky and back into Tennessee. *Ibid.*, #1.

5   William Rosecrans (1819-1898) took command of

the new Army of the Cumberland and was given the task of pursuing Bragg in the struggle for control of the region (Middle Tennessee). After gathering supplies at Nashville in case his communications should be cut, Rosecrans moved towards Murfreesboro where Bragg awaited him. Despite his numerical advantage Rosecrans was pressed hard by the Confederates and only by sheer determination did he prevent defeat during the first day's fighting. After Bragg's withdrawal Rosecrans turned Murfreesboro into a strong, well-supplied fortress. *Stones River*, National Park Service, U. S. Department of the Interior.

6 According to information given to me by Greg Leaming of Rogersville, Tennessee, found in Peter Cozzens' book, *No Better Place to Die* (University of Illinois Press, 1990), the 38th Illinois is mentioned three times. This diary (William Patterson's) neatly complements this book. William E. Patterson was on the right wing of the army during the Battle of Stones River. Colonel Henry Leaming was commanding the 40th Indiana on the left wing. They both encountered troops under Maj. Gen. A. P. Stewart. One of Stewart's ancestors also lives in Rogersville.

7 On December 26, 1862, Rosecrans, with 45,000 men, moved out of Nashville, intending to sweep Bragg and his force of 38,000 aside and drive on to Chattanooga. Four days later Federal forces neared Murfreesboro. Bragg's army had been found. *Stones River,* National Park Service, U. S. Department of the Interior.

8   This engagement was between General Joseph Wheeler's cavalry and Brigadier General George Maney's brigade on the Confederate side against skirmish lines put out by the advancing Federal army under Major General William S. Rosecrans. Maney's brigade was the Third Brigade of Major General William S. Rosecrans. Maney's brigade was the Third Brigade of Major General Benjamin Cheatham's division, Polk's corps. Johnson and Buel (eds.), *Battles and Leaders*, III, 611.

9   December 31. Very early this morning a very hard fight commenced on the left wing & the enemy giving back it continued to increas very fast. About 8. o.clock we being in the centre the time came for us to advance & there being a yankey battery just in front of us we had it to charge upon & in so doing we soon frightened the enemy & makeing them leave it we took posesion of it. In this struggle we had a great many men wounded & some few killed the enemies' loss bing fuly as heavy as of our own, we then followed on after the enemy capturing several pieces of artilery & a greateal of other Government property. Driveing the enemy about two miles & being relieved by other troops we retired from the field returning back to our stand & haveing fires we slep very comfortable during the night. Robert Masten Holmes, C.S.A., *Kemper County Rebel*, (University and College Press of Mississippi, Jackson, 1973), 38.

10   Thousands of Union troops burst from the cedars located across the field and were followed closely by victory-confident Confederates. The Chicago Board of

Trade Battery, so called because the Board of Trade provided the money for establishing and equipping the 6-gun battery, sprang into action. Their charges of canister forced the Confederates to withdraw to the cedars. A second battery joined in on the left, and the combined fire broke up the attack. *Ibid*

11   At the Battle of Stone's River, Tennessee, in January, 1863, the Federal infantry in three days exhausted over 2,000,000 rounds of ammunition, and the artillery fired 20,307 rounds. The total weight of the projectiles was in excess of 375,000 pounds. William H. Price, *The Civil War Handbook,* (Fairfax, Virginia, 1961), 12.

12   From December 31, 1862 to January 2, 1863, the Union total losses (killed, wounded, missing) were 11,578 men, the Confederate total losses were 25,560 men. *Ibid.,* 67.

13   Vallandigham, once considered as candidate for Governor of Ohio, was an outspoken critic of the North in the war. He was tried by a military commission, found guilty, and ordered imprisoned "insome fortress in the United States" for the balance of the war. Lincoln commuted Vallandigham's sentence, ordering him sent, not to prison, but into the Confederacy. On May 25 Federal cavalry took Vallandigham through Rosecrans' lines near Murfreesboro and turned him over to surprised Confederate pickets, who hastily sought guidance from the rear and then, lacking anything better to do, accepted their

charge. Bruce Catton, *Never Call Retreat* (Washington Square Press, New York, 1965), 164-166.

14 Rosecrans, by rapid and forced marches, brought up his troops from Crawfish Springs. Bragg ordered his left wing divisions to cross to the west side of the Chickamauga. "Chickamauga and Chattanooga Battlefields," *National Park Service Historical Handbook Series No. 25* (Washington, D. C., 1956), 18.

15 "Captain: I have the honor to report the part taken by the Thirty-eighth Illinois Infantry in the battle of the 19th and 20th of September, near Crawfish Spring. September 18 broke camp near Dug Gap about dark; marched about 4 miles to the left, relieving General Brannan's division. On the 19th moved to the left about 10 o'clock. Passed Crawfish Spring about 3 miles and filed right into the woods, double-quicked about a mile and a quarter, filed right and formed on the left, by file into line, on the right of Colonel Heg's brigade. The regiment was under a very heavy fire; were ordered to lie down. Company K was lying in the road and was very much exposed; they suffered severely. The men, ordered not to fire, stood their ground without flinching. In a short time the men were ordered to their feet and the line was moved forward; the right and left became entangled with other regiments. For a few moments the firing was heavy, when it became evident that the troops on our left had given way, exposing the left flank. We were ordered to fall back, which we did, firing as we went, to a

road at the edge of the timber, where a stand was made till, being heavily pressed on the left and front, the line retired across an open field to the woods. Here the men rallied at a fence, the batteries playing over their heads. The enemy was checked. A line was formed and charged across the open field to the woods from where we were first driven, and held it under a heavy fire until a brigade of General Sheridan's division came to our relief. The regiment was then reformed and bivouacked in an open field rear of the battlefield. The regiment entered the fight at 2 o'clock and was relieved at half past 5; loss very heavy." Report of Capt. William C. Harris, Thirty-eighth Illinois Infantry, Chattanooga, Tenn., September 28, 1863.

Appendix

There are three items contained in this appendix: two letters that William wrote to his parents while he was fighting in the Civil War, and one item that was added to his diary, sort of as an afterthought. This additional item is a "Short History of Jasper County, Illinois," which he apparently decided to write after he had returned home. It seems as if, after he had the inspiration to write such a document he was in search of something to write upon, or in, and his eyes fell upon his Civil War diary. Some of the pages were blank at the end of the diary, so....

These items are presented here with much of the original language, spelling, and punctuation intact. Some restructuring of the letters and history has been done to facilitate reading.

Near Corinth Mississippi

June 1st [1862]

Dear Father

I write these lines to inform you that I am well and hope this will find you all well. We are camped at present several miles from Corinth and just outside of the rebel fortifications about half a mile to the left of the Mobile railroad waiting "further orders." I presume you have ere this heard the particulars of the battle I wish to merely add that the victorious 38th has marched through the fortifications of Corinth "Nor cost a single man."

The fighting commenced on the 28th. We had left Hamburg and were camped about 6 miles from farmington. In the morning the artillery opened on the line. We had only time to put two days rations of hard crackers and raw bacon in our haver sacks and then we marched off only asking to get a sight at the rebs, but we was disappointed.

We were sent to the extreme left of Pope's division and took our place with the 21st still under Carlin's command in a ditch or rifle pit I believe they call it and remained there till the 31st. We were held as a reserve, with the 1st Mo Battery. On the 30th Corinth was evacuated. There was not much fighting on either side. A pretty constant cannonading was kept up on our right with an occasional infantry skirmish.

On the 31st we started in pursuit of the secesh our advance have overtaken them about three miles ahead. They was acrofsed a creek down here and burned the bridge. Our men were constructing a bridge, probably a pontoon bridge, which will soon be complete and we will be within...

Ten deserters came to our camp near farmington on the 27th. They were Mifsourians of Fredericktown "fame" and were sick of the "cause." They said they had heard that General Carlin had reinforced Walleck with ten thousand regulars.

I have just come from a rebel camp about half a mile from here. They had fled in such haste that they had left their tents, wagons, provisions, cooking utensils, &c. Every thing had been burned but their tents or partly burned. A great many guns had .... and left.

I haven't received a letter from any of you for lo these many days and I would be mity glad to hear from you. Yours truly

W E Patterson

Camp[ed] before Murfreesboro

January 5th A.D. 1863

Dear Father - I again have the opportunity to write to you. Since we left Nashville I have been in three fights and have came out without a scratch or the lofs of a thing through the protection of a higher Power.

We fought at Nolensville on the 26th of December. Minor Mitchell was killed there and Ed Rofs also killed and Gimore, Blifs, George Stockwell and Andy Berlin wounded. We drove the enemy from Nolensville to knob Gap 3 miles. There they had a battery of 8 guns supported by a strong force of dismounted cavalry. Our brigade charged a mile and a half in[to] the fire of the battery and cavalry and took one piece of artillery. Davis and Carlin say they never saw such a charge before.

We attacked the enemy here first on the 30th, and the 31st. We had to skedaddle but we can't be blamed when the Pea Ridge men run first. We commenced the attack about 2 o'clock P.M. on the 30th and fought till dark the enemy being posted behind a fence. The 21st and 15th Regiments were engaged as skirmishers. Our regiment and the 101st in reserve.

Next morning at daylight the rebels attacked us. The 3rd Brigade pea ridge men were about 100 yard before us to the left. They fought over a strip of about 30 yards an hour and a half, retreating and advancing under a constant storm of balls. They they run back through our left and we took some of the 3rd Brigade and rallied behind us and we drove them back on the left wing. At this time every regiment escept the 38th was in retreat and the rebs began to turn our right. Davis sent the order to retreat but his orderly instead of riding among the bullets and giving the order only gave it to the right wing and the first we knew Cos I and K on the left were alone so we followed the example and brought up the rear. We were fighting in a thick cedar swamp and the rebs sheltered themselves among the trees. I was about the center of the company a-blazing away with all my might at a squad of rebs behind a clump of little cedars. I watched till one stepped out to fire and then I would pop away at him. I looked round and the 38th was skedaddling like turks and I skedaddled after them. Many of them threw away their knapsacks and ran for life.

We had to cross a cornfield and then a cotton field in which numbers of our men fell. I didn't throw anything away but when I got tired of running I walked. I can say that I staid with the flag the whole day and whenever an attempt was made to rally I was with them.

We retreated about a mile and then formed the 15th Wisconsin and our regiment into one, numbering in all about 200 men. We took our position behind a fence and fought a while, but the rebs kept advancing, pouring a tide of lead in amongst us and we were forced to retreat again, but Company K the last to leave the fence. We fell back to the railroad where old Rosencrans led the charge. (illegible)...know are Lieutenant...Rienza, John McDowell, Burnside finger, and them ... Christian, J W Brooks, Bill Jourd, slightly, there are several missing Eliphaz Reisner taken prisoner and paroled. ... Moulden wants me to say that he is well and he is going to write home. Old Henceforth was as cool as a cucumber all the time. I have a great mind to name some of your acquaintances that acted with the most bravery [and] were the first [to] rally around the old regimental colors. They are Henry Blifs, H.P. Moulden, I. P. Devine, David Bowers, Frank Carter, that stuck to the flag through the hottest. Me and Tawalt Bower retreated acrofs the cotton field together, taking our time to it and others throwing away their knapsacks and making (illegible) effortlessly. George Wander...is missing. I heard that he was run over by a horse and is at Nashville. Minor Mitchell...who was shot. I went back and...was over him could not talk...he suffered much he replied...he could not be...not live...if he is not he was...

A large force of fresh troops to our relief with a strong artillery piece. Then the fighting was desparate. Grape, canister and rifle balls flew like hail and the rebels were driven back. After the fight Company K numbered 27 men, the 38th reg 127, the 15th 70 men.

New Year's day the rebels again attacked our Brigade but only six companies of skirmishers were engaged and Company K was among them. We were advanced to a ridge in front of our line, six companies of us, numbering in all not more than 120 men. A large grey Eagle set upon a large oak over our heads and looked quietly down upon us as we fought (was it a token?). A whole Brigade of rebels advanced and poured in the pickle. They advanced to 100 yards or so, meeting only our fire and one of Sheridan's batteries and then broke and ran, more than skedaddled, numbers of them laid down to excape our bullets and then surrendered, including a lieutenant. On the 2nd the rebels attacked on the left acrofs the river and we went to reinforce them, but the rebs were driven back before we got there. Yesterday morning we came back here, wading the river. Now the battle is ended and Murfreesboro is ours. Lieutenant Scott is wounded, O.S. Reed wounded mortally. It is thought and I know not who all Henry Moore, Uncle Joab are prisoners.

W. E. Patterson

A Short History of Jasper County, Illinois

The county of Jasper was organized in 1836 or 37 from portions of Crawford and Clay. Newton was then located on the Land of Benjamin Reynolds in the portion taken from Crawford County. John Barnes was clerk of both courts in Jasper Co. Lewis W. Jordan, sheriff, L. D. Wade, Treasurer. Justin Harlan first circuit Judge of 4th Judicial circuit. first court held at this time in the house of Sheriff Jordan. A hewn log house was built on the present school house lot for a court House, school house, church, etc, etc. The first county court was composed of Wm Bridges, Judge of Probate; Hiram Wade, circuit and county clerk; and three county commifsioners and county recorder. the present court house was built or finished in 1845 by Eli Curtis. a hewn log Jail stood in the south west corner of the court House Square from a period lost in the mists of antiquity until about the year 1854 when a stone jail was built in the hollow north of the court House and near the river by George Bains.

the first settlement in the county was in the dark bend. The
first pioneers were the Enlows, Crabtrees, Bogards, Powells,
etc.

first settlers of Granville Township [were] Clemmons,
Groves, Metheny, Mill. [first settlers of] Willow Hill [were]
Eaton, Doty, Allison. [The] first mill in the county was
Eaton's on the North Fork Crooked Creed. [first settlers of)
Hannatta [were] Ray, Stepen, Musgrove, Swick. of Gorve
[Grove?] Arnold, Wagle, VanDyke, Shy, Peckenfa.

[first settlers of] North Muddy [were] Anderson, Choat,
Reynolds, Autry, Stevens. [Of] South Muddy and
Smallwood; Cathers, Evans, Mashes, Hoovers, Hanna's.

[Of] St. Marie; Underhill, Qualls, Sturgeons, McCullies.

Voting was all done at Newton till about 1852 when the
county was divided into precincts and about 1855 Township
organization was adopted.

Up to 1840 Jasper Co. was little more than an unbroken
wilderness till 1845 but little of the land had been entered,

the settlers being mostly squatters. by 1852 the public land
was all taken up.

About from 1842 to 1845 the families of the Brookses,
Chapmans, Kiblers, Cummins and other Colonies [Coloni-
zers?] came to Jasper about 1837. the Picquets and
Schifferteins settled St. Marie.

in the year 1851 Jasper County had but few roads that
deserved the name. the Palestine and Olney or Maysville
road and the Louisville road might be mentioned. the State
road from Newton to Granville and Martinsville was
surveyed in 1851.

Index

B. Parker.

Bostick, Lindsay: enlistment, brother to Tower Bostick, 2.

Bostick, Tower: enlistment, brother to Lindsay Bostick, 2.

Bowers, David: enlistment, 2; "stuck to the flag through the hottest," at the battle of Stones River, 83.

Bowers, Michael: David's brother, enlistment, 2.

Brackett, Raleigh M: enlistment, 2; missing or deserted at the conclusion of the battle of Stones River, 42.

Brewer, Cyrus J: enlistment, 2.

Bridges, Boss M: enlistment, 2; taken prisoner at the battle of Stones River, 42; paroled, returned home, 68.

Bridges, Matthew H: enlistment, 2.

Brooks, G. M: enlistment, 2; returned home, 68.

Brooks, John W: enlistment, 2; slightly [wounded] at the battle of Murfreesboro, 82.

Brooks, Lewis: enlistment, 2.

Burnside, Anderson: enlistment, 2; wounded at the battle of Stones River, 42; mentioned, possibly dead, 82.

Carter, Frank: enlistment, 2; "that stuck to the flag through the hottest," at the battle of Stones River, 83; returned home, 68.

Cather(s), Ezra: *may have been brother to Nathan, not mentioned in first enlistment*, 1-2; returned home, 68.

Cathers, Nathan: enlistment, 2; returned home, 68.

Chestnut, John 1: enlistment, 2.

Christian, Martin: enlistment, 2; wounded slightly at the battle of Stones River, 42, 82.

Clark, Ithamar: enlistment, 2.

Colvin, William: enlistment, 2; discharged from the service, 8-9.

Debolt, Jonah F: enlistment, 2.

Devine, James D: enlistment, 2; "stuck to the flag through the hottest," at the battle of Stones River, 83.

Dillman, William: *not mentioned in the original enl-*

istment, *may have joined later*, 1-2; returned home, 68.

Dobbins, Elzy: enlistment, 2.

Dyer, Dyson: (not mentioned in enlistments), 2; died at Camp Butler, Missouri on January 1, 1862, buried on the Farmington Road, Missouri, 7.

Elder, Richard: enlistment, 2.

Fiesey, Jonas: enlistment, 2.

Fithian, Job: enlistment, 2.

Foster, Jonathon: enlistment, 2.

Foster, Zed: enlistment, 2.

Four, Lew: enlistment, 2.

Francis, John: enlistment, 2.

Freeman, James E: enlistment, 2.

Hagerman, John (Zug): enlistment, 2.

Hankins, Avery: enlistment, brother to David Hankins, 2; wounded at the Battle of Stones River, 42.

Hankins, David B: enlistment, 1861, 2.

Harris, Bushrod: enlistment, 2; received commission of 1st Lieutenant, 7; returned home, 68.

Harris, Joe W: enlist, 2.

Hawkins, Martin B: enlistment, 2; died at Pilot Knob, Missouri, 7.

Hensly, George: enlistment, 2.

Hibler, G. W: enlistment, 2.

Holm, Jerry: enlistment, 2.

Irving, A. I: enlistment, 2; discharged from service, 9.

Jones, John L: enlistment, 2.

Jordan, William: enlistment , 2.

Kibler, Sydney: enlistment, 2.

Kinney, Joe: enlistment, 2.

Lee, John W: enlistment 2; wounded at the Battle of Stones River, 42.

Lord, William: enlistment, 2.

Malcolm, John R. enlistment 2.

Martin, William: enlistment, 2; died near Corinth, Mississippi, buried on the Jacinto Road, 12.

McDowell, John Lee: enlistment, 2; wounded at the battle of Stones River, 42; mentioned in letter, 82.

McNair, Joe: enlistment, 2.

Mitchell, Minor: enlistment, 2; fell, pierced through the breast with a piece of shell at the battle of Stones River, 38, 81; last words, 83.

Mondon, Decatur: enlistment, 2.

Moore, Henry C: enlistment, 2; taken prisoner at the battle of Stones River, 42; mentioned in letter, 84.

Moulden, H. P: enlistment, brother to Joe P. Moulden, 2; "wants me to say that he is well and he is going to write home. Old Henceforth was as cool as a cucumber all the time," 82; "stuck to the flag through the hottest," at the battle of Stones River, 83.

Moulden, Joe P: brother to H. P. Moulden, enlistment, 2.

Mulvany, John: enlistment, 2.

Newton, Kenneth: enlistment, 2.

Parker, Napoleon Bonaparte: enlistment, 2; returned home, 68.

Patterson, W. E: dedication, v; construction of original diary of, vii; biography of, xi; acknowledgment of, xii; enlistment, 2; at hospital at Ironton, Missouri, 8; wounded at the Battle of Chickamauga, 65; taken prisoner, paroled, 65; at hospital in Nashville, 67;

mustered out of U. S. service, arrived at home, 68.

Ping, Robert: enlistment 2; returned home, 68.

Powell, Joseph; enlistment 2; taken prisoner, 42.

Reed, Jacob A: enlistment, 2.

Reed, Jacob E: enlistment, 2.

Reisner, Eliphaz: enlistment, 2; taken prisoner, paroled, 42; returned home, 68.

Richards, D. W: enlistment, 2.

Richards, Stephen: enlistment, 2; discharged from service, 8.

Riggin, Lewis G: enlistment, 2.

Rosebalt, Frederic: enlistment, 2.

Rotzler, Frederick: enlistment 2.

Ryan, Wickham: enlistment, 2.

Scott, Peter Neal: enlistment, 2; elected 2nd Lieutenant, Co. K, 7.

Scott, Sam: enlistment, 2; returned home, 68.

Selby, A. P: enlistment, 2; died at Pilot Knob, 7.

Shedelbauer, Joe: enlistment, 2.

Smith, Isaac: enlistment, 2; discharged from service, 9.

Stallings, Benjamin: enlistment, 2.

Stewart, Assistant Surgeon: enlistment, 2.

Stockwell, George W: brother to Michael, enlistment, 2; wounded, 38, 81.

Stockwell, Michael: brother to George, enlistment, 2. 39; returned home, 68.

Sturgis, Sergeant Major: enlistment and election of, 2.

Sutton, G. W: enlistment, 2.

Sutton, William: enlistment, 2.

Teed, Surgeon: enlistment and election of, 2.

Trexler, John: enlistment, 2.

Trexler, Jonathon: enlistment, 2; returned home, 68.

Vanderhogg, George V: enlistment, 2.

Walters, Elias (Pony): enlisted, brother to Powell, 2.

Walters, Powell: enlisted, brother to Elias, 2; died at Pilot Knob, Missouri, body sent home, 7.

Welch, Ross: enlistment, 2.

Welch, William: enlistment, 2.

Wheeler, A: enlistment, brother to Zebulon, 2.

Wheeler, Zebulon P: enlistment, brother to A. Wheeler, 2; died at Pilot Knob, Missouri, body sent home, 7.

Willet, Adjutant W: enlistment, selected as regimental officer, 3.

Wilson, Martin B: enlistment, 2; discharged from service, 9.

Worthy, Elijah: enlistment, brother to William, 2; returned home, 68.

Worthy, William: enlistment, brother to Elijah, 2; returned home, 68.

Other Officers:

Alden, Major H. N: in command of 38th Regiment, 47: changed his command, comment of soldier about, 50.

Asboth, Gen: command of, at Corinth, Mississippi, 12.

Beaufort, Brig. Gen. Hamilton: forces of, at Corinth, Mississippi, 12.

Brown, Col: of the 1st Indiana Cavalry, in command of the 3rd Brigade, 8.

killed General Nelson, 22; his division commanded by Mitchell, 25; at Nashville, Tennessee, 34; 1st Division, 35; ordered to the left at Stones River, 43; at Franklin, Tennessee, 44; as general, went on scouting mission, 45; at Liberty Gap, 48; divisional meeting, 54; mentioned, 81; order to retreat at Nolensville, Tennessee, 82.

Fuller, F: Quartermaster, 3.

Gavit, Maj: killed while leading a charge, 5.

Gilmer, Maj. Daniel: regimental officer of 26th Illinois, 3; detachment started to Potosi, 4; commanded the 38th as Lieut. Col., 26; selected brushy spot, 55.

Heg, Col. Hans C: commanded 15th Wisconsin Infantry, 13; made a stand at Stones River, 41; commanded Carlin's Brigade, 45; commanded 3rd Brigade, 48.

Hotchkiss, Capt: commanded 2nd Minnesota Battery, 13; took position at Salt River, commanded 2nd Brigade, 8.

Johnson, Gov. Andrew: military governor of Tennessee, 6.

Loomis, Col: commanded 26th Illinois Regiment, 3.

McCook, Gen. Alexander McDowell: division went to Nashville, 16; passed the 38th at Edgefield, 16; at Bowling Green, Kentucky, 18; commanded by, 35; commanded right wing of army, 40; mentioned, 54.

McKee, Lt. Col: of the 15th Wisconsin, 32; skirmish with mounted squad, 34; death wish, killed at Stones River, 41.

Mitchell, Captain: commanded 16th Ohio Battery (later killed at Vicksburg), 8; battery, 9.

Mitchell, Gen. Robert: took command of division at Eastport, 13; lefft Bowling Green, 18; retained command of Davis' Division, 22; division at Perryville, 25; placed division in line of battle, 26; left division, 29; enthusiastically cheer-

absent at Perryville, 26; resigned at Rolling Fork, 41.

Pease, Col: provost marshal of the division, 17.

Pitcher, Col: commander of Camp Butler, Illinois, 3.

Rosecrans, Gen. William S: took command of the Army of the Cumberland, division reviewed by, 34, 72; suspended operations, 39; passed, leading a charge of Rousseau's division, 42, 82; referred to as "the Dutchman" by rebels, 53; moved toward Murfreesboro, pressed hard, turned Murfreesboro into a strong, well-supplied fortress, with 45,000 men, 73; Valandigham sent through lines of, rapid and forced marches of, 75; confederates engaged a-gainst, 76.

Steel, Gen: commander of military district of Missouri, 8.

Stern, Col: commander of the 101st Ohio, 21.

Vallandigham, Clement L: the "Great Banished," 48; candidate for governor of Ohio, 74; Lincoln com-

brigade broke ranks, 41.

Places and Battles:

Bowling Green, Kentucky: on the pike leading to, 16; McCook's division four miles from, 18; arrived at Buell left, camped at, 19 march to, 21; supply train left at, 28; chapter title started for, arrival, 31.

Camp Butler, Illinois: on the train for, arrival at, went into camp at, 1; prepared to leave, marched out of 3; Dyson Dyer died at Washington Johnson relinquished position at, 7.

Cape Girardeau, Missouri: joined by Col. Plummer's command at, 4; camped 27 miles from, arrived at, 11.

Chaplin Hills (Perryville, Kentucky) : chapter title, the battle of, first gun fired in, 25; camped south of, 31.

Chattanooga, Tennessee: moved towards, 58; Chattanooga Road, 60; approached 61; rebels retreated from, 64; started towards, 68; Rosecrans drove on to, 73; mentioned, 75; Capt. Harris' battle report, 76.

banks of, 61.

Corinth, Mississippi (also Shiloh, Pittsburgh Landing): on our way to, in front of, 11; rebels evacuated, Price's Camp three miles from, Clear Creek four or five miles from, retreat toward, 12; Grant had his men at, the main Confederate force at, 71.

Crawfish Spring: in hospital at, 65; Rosecrans brought his troops to, battle near, passed, 75.

Cumberland Mountains: went to camp at the foot of, 54; climbed the, 55.

Cumberland River: crossed, 16.

Edgefield (Edgfield [sic]), or Edgefield Junction, Tennessee: camped at, forces passed us at, 16; junction of Louisville and Nashville (Railroad), 17; went into camp at, 31; opposite Nashville, marched to, 34.

Florence, Alabama: started for, arrived at, a beautiful town, 14; march extended from, 21.

Franklin, Tennessee: left Nashville Road at, 15;

Pike, rebels in force at, 34; Bragg outposts at, 35; Davis' division started toward, 44; camped seven miles from, arrived at, Provost Guard in, infantry left at, 45.

Fredericktown, Missouri: Jeff Thompson's command at, marched out toward, 4; rebels in position at, 5; Col. Lowe killed at, 8.

Gettysburg, Virginia: official dispatch of the defeat of Lee at, 54.

Hamburg Landing, Tennessee: landed at, marched from, 11.

Jacksonport, Arkansas: Van Dorn had gone to, camped at a log cabin church eight miles from, arrived at, Gen. Curtis' command at, 10.

Lancaster, Kentucky: arrived at, rebels in force at, 28; rebels retreated from, 29.

Lookout Mountain: camped at foot of, foraging excursion to the top of, crossed, marched onto, 57.

Louisville, Kentucky: started on the march to, 16; rebel army marching toward, the main army marched toward, 18; Bragg moved on toward, 19; rebel army turned right to, camped eleven miles below, 20; arrived at, 21; forced march from Florence, Alabama to, welcome of citizens at, remained four days at army reinforced at, 21; Gen. Davis killed Gen. Nelson at, left Louisville, 22; sent to exchange barracks in, headed home from, 68.

Murfreesboro, Tennessee: arrived at, 16; intermission at, 21; the rebels under Bragg at, 35; rebels evacuate, 37; marched towards, rebel lines in front of, 39; camped about four miles from, 43; moved camp two miles south of, 44; nine miles from, 46; moved camp one mile from, 47; camped compactly around, 48; Rosecrans moved toward, Rosecrans turned into a strong fortress, Federal forces neared (on December 30, 1862), 73; camped before, 81; M. is ours, 84.

Nashville, Tennessee: started towards, 14; Road, 15; a N., marched through, 16 Edgefield Junction ten miles from, 17; marched towards, 31; Gen. Jeff C Davis arrived at, moved camp four miles south of 34; rebels thirty-two miles from, 35; guarded a supply train going to, 44; applied for certificate of parole at returning to service stayed at, 68; Rosecrans gathered supplies at, moved out of, 73; heard George Wander is at, 83.

Perryville, Kentucky: see *Chaplin Hills, the battle of.*

Pilot Knob, Missouri: took the Iron Mountain Railroad to, arrived at, 3; camped in a field near, forces at, 4; left for Sulphur Springs, heavy artillery at, 6; the 38th left, Wheeler, Selby, Hawkins, Hensley and Walters died at, 7.

Pocahontas, Arkansas: marched towards, 9; moved camp one mile west of, left and marched ten miles, flat boat pressed into service at, 10.

Shelbyville, Tennessee: Bragg retreated to, 44.

Stevenson, Alabama: marched to, camped on railroad west of, guerrillas around, 55; arrived at (on way home), 68.

Stones River: camped on banks of, 16; Chapter Title, the battle of, 37; "quiet on," 40; crossed, end of battle, recrossed, 43; later camped on, 48; footnotes concerning, 72-74.

Tennessee River: at Fort Henry on the, 11; marched to Eastport on the, 13; Florence on the, 14; marched to Caperton's Ferry on the, 55.

Tullahoma, Tennessee: marched to, 53.

Vicksburg, Mississippi: Capt. Mitchell killed at, 8; official dispatch of the surrender of, 54.

www.ingramcontent.com/pod-product-compliance
Lightning Source LLC
Chambersburg PA
CBHW071057090426
42737CB00013B/2358